KING PENGUIN

COLLECTED

Geoffrey Hill was [...] shire, in 1932, the son [...] to 1952 his home wa[...] village of Fairfield. He was educ[...] village school, at the County High School, Bromsgrove, and at Keble College, Oxford (which elected him into an honorary fellowship in 1981). Having taken a First in English he taught for many years at the University of Leeds. In 1981 he moved to Cambridge where he is a University Lecturer in English and a Fellow of Emmanuel College. He is the author of five books of poetry and a volume of critical essays. His version of Ibsen's *Brand* was produced at the National Theatre in 1978.

It is now more than thirty years since Geoffrey Hill first attracted attention with the earliest poems collected here. From time to time his poetry has won prizes and the word 'greatness' finds its way into the occasional press-notice. More often, though, the work of this 'masterly and compelling poet', 'a poet at once urgent and timeless', has encountered either baffled goodwill or baffled resentment ('unbearable, bullying, intransigent, intolerant, brilliant', 'inaccessibly obscure and strange and mannered', 'immense, baffling talent', 'mandarin and rarefied', 'toil and artifice', 'sick grandeur', 'glowering, unlovely egotism', 'warmth in these poems is like a dying sun seen through a wall of ice').

Since hostile and favourable reviewers alike concede Hill's 'tremendous forcefulness and simplicity', the power of his 'authentic and authoritative voice', it is difficult to understand the reason for so much dislike. It is evident, however, that this poetry – 'never condescending for the sake of yielding instant meaning, keeping aloof from superficialities of fashion and true to its imaginative temper and purposes' – has disturbed the literary consensus for three decades.

# GEOFFREY HILL

## COLLECTED POEMS

**A KING PENGUIN**

**PUBLISHED BY PENGUIN BOOKS**

Penguin Books Ltd, Harmondsworth, Middlesex, England
Viking Penguin Inc., 40 West 23rd Street, New York, New York 10010, U.S.A.
Penguin Books Australia Ltd, Ringwood, Victoria, Australia
Penguin Books Canada Ltd, 2801 John Street, Markham, Ontario, Canada L3R 1B4
Penguin Books (N.Z.) Ltd, 182–190 Wairau Road, Auckland 10, New Zealand

*For the Unfallen*, *King Log*, *Mercian Hymns*, *Tenebrae* and *The Mystery of the Charity
of Charles Péguy* first published by André Deutsch 1959, 1968, 1971, 1978 and 1983
This collection first published by Penguin Books 1985
Reprinted 1987

Printed and bound in Great Britain by
Cox & Wyman Ltd, Reading

Typeset in Linotron Bembo with Caslon display
by Rowland Phototypesetting Ltd, Bury St Edmunds, Suffolk

# CONTENTS

## FOR THE UNFALLEN (1959)

# KING LOG (1968)

# MERCIAN HYMNS (1971)

## TENEBRAE (1978)

## HYMNS TO OUR LADY OF CHARTRES (1984)

## THE MYSTERY OF THE CHARITY OF CHARLES PÉGUY (1983)

*How is the gold become dim! how is the most fine gold changed! the stones of the sanctuary are poured out in the top of every street*

LAMENTATIONS 4:1

*Quand le monde moderne avilit, mettons que c'est alors qu'il travaille de sa partie*

CHARLES PÉGUY

*In the gloom, the gold gathers the light against it*

EZRA POUND

# FOR THE UNFALLEN

# GENESIS

## I

Against the burly air I strode
Crying the miracles of God.

And first I brought the sea to bear
Upon the dead weight of the land;
And the waves flourished at my prayer,
The rivers spawned their sand.

And where the streams were salt and full
The tough pig-headed salmon strove,
Ramming the ebb, in the tide's pull,
To reach the steady hills above.

## II

The second day I stood and saw
The osprey plunge with triggered claw,
Feathering blood along the shore,
To lay the living sinew bare.

And the third day I cried: 'Beware
The soft-voiced owl, the ferret's smile,
The hawk's deliberate stoop in air,
Cold eyes, and bodies hooped in steel,
Forever bent upon the kill.'

## III

And I renounced, on the fourth day,
This fierce and unregenerate clay,

Building as a huge myth for man
The watery Leviathan,

And made the long-winged albatross
Scour the ashes of the sea
Where Capricorn and Zero cross,
A brooding immortality –
Such as the charmed phoenix has
In the unwithering tree.


IV

The phoenix burns as cold as frost;
And, like a legendary ghost,
The phantom-bird goes wild and lost,
Upon a pointless ocean tossed.

So, the fifth day, I turned again
To flesh and blood and the blood's pain.


V

On the sixth day, as I rode
In haste about the works of God,
With spurs I plucked the horse's blood.

By blood we live, the hot, the cold,
To ravage and redeem the world:
There is no bloodless myth will hold.

And by Christ's blood are men made free
Though in close shrouds their bodies lie
Under the rough pelt of the sea;

Though Earth has rolled beneath her weight
The bones that cannot bear the light.

# GOD'S LITTLE MOUNTAIN

Below, the river scrambled like a goat
Dislodging stones. The mountain stamped its foot,
Shaking, as from a trance. And I was shut
With wads of sound into a sudden quiet.

I thought the thunder had unsettled heaven,
All was so still. And yet the sky was riven
By flame that left the air cold and engraven.
I waited for the word that was not given,

Pent up into a region of pure force,
Made subject to the pressure of the stars;
I saw the angels lifted like pale straws;
I could not stand before those winnowing eyes

And fell, until I found the world again.
Now I lack grace to tell what I have seen;
For though the head frames words the tongue has none.
And who will prove the surgeon to this stone?

# HOLY THURSDAY

Naked, he climbed to the wolf's lair;
He beheld Eden without fear,
Finding no ambush offered there
But sleep under the harbouring fur.

He said: 'They are decoyed by love
Who, tarrying through the hollow grove,
Neglect the seasons' sad remove.
Child and nurse walk hand in glove

As unaware of Time's betrayal,
Weaving their innocence with guile.
But they must cleave the fire's peril
And suffer innocence to fall.

I have been touched with that fire,
And have fronted the she-wolf's lair.
Lo, she lies gentle and innocent of desire
Who was my constant myth and terror.'

# MERLIN

I will consider the outnumbering dead:
For they are the husks of what was rich seed.
Now, should they come together to be fed,
They would outstrip the locusts' covering tide.

Arthur, Elaine, Mordred; they are all gone
Among the raftered galleries of bone.
By the long barrows of Logres they are made one,
And over their city stands the pinnacled corn.

# THE BIDDEN GUEST

The starched unbending candles stir
As though a wind had caught their hair,
As though the surging of a host
Had charged the air of Pentecost.
And I believe in the spurred flame,
Those racing tongues, but cannot come
Out of my heart's unbroken room;
Nor feel the lips of fire among
The cold light and the chilling song,
The broken mouths that spill their hoard
Of prayer like beads on to a board.
There, at the rail, each muffled head
Swings sombrely. O quiet deed.
This is the breaking of the bread;
On this the leanest heart may feed
When by the stiffly-linened priest
All wounds of light are newly dressed,
Healed by the pouring-in of wine
From bitter as from sweet grapes bled.
But one man lay beneath his vine
And, waking, found that it was dead.
And so my heart has ceased to breathe
(Though there God's worm blunted its head
And stayed.) And still I seem to smile.
Wounds have thick lips and cannot tell
If there is blackness couched beneath.
'Yet there are wounds, unquenched with oil,
And blazing eyes that would compel
Evil to turn, though like a mole
It dug blind alleys down the soil.'
So I heard once. But now I hear,
Like shifted blows at my numb back,
A grinding heel; a scraped chair.

The heart's tough shell is still to crack
When, spent of all its wine and bread,
Unwinkingly the altar lies
Wreathed in its sour breath, cold and dead.
A server has put out its eyes.

# IN MEMORY
# OF JANE FRASER

When snow like sheep lay in the fold
And winds went begging at each door,
And the far hills were blue with cold,
And a cold shroud lay on the moor,

She kept the siege. And every day
We watched her brooding over death
Like a strong bird above its prey.
The room filled with the kettle's breath.

Damp curtains glued against the pane
Sealed time away. Her body froze
As if to freeze us all, and chain
Creation to a stunned repose.

She died before the world could stir.
In March the ice unloosed the brook
And water ruffled the sun's hair.
Dead cones upon the alder shook.

# THE TURTLE DOVE

Love that drained her drained him she'd loved, though each
For the other's sake forged passion upon speech,
Bore their close days through sufferance towards night
Where she at length grasped sleep and he lay quiet

As though needing no questions, now, to guess
What her secreting heart could not well hide.
Her caught face flinched in half-sleep at his side.
Yet she, by day, modelled her real distress,

Poised, turned her cheek to the attending world
Of children and intriguers and the old;
Conversed freely, exercised, was admired,
Being strong to dazzle. All this she endured

To affront him. He watched her rough grief work
Under the formed surface of habit. She spoke
Like one long undeceived but she was hurt.
She denied more love, yet her starved eyes caught

His, devouring, at times. Then, as one self-dared,
She went to him, plied there; like a furious dove
Bore down with visitations of such love
As his lithe, fathoming heart absorbed and buried.

# THE TROUBLESOME REIGN

So much he had from fashion and no more:
Her trained hard gaze, brief lips whose laughter spat
Concession to desire. She suffered that,
Feeding a certain green-fuel to his fire.

Reluctant heat! This burning of the dead
Could consume her also. She moved apart
As if, through such denial, he might be made
Himself again familiar and unscarred,

Contained, even wary, though not too much
To take pleasure considering her flesh shone,
Her salt-worn summer dress. But he had gone
Thirty days through such a dream of taste and touch

When the sun stood for him and the violent larks
Stabbed up into the sun. She was his, then;
Her limbs grasped him, satisfied, while his brain
Judged every move and cry from its separate dark.

More dark, more separate, now, yet still not dead,
Their mouths being drawn to public and private speech –
Though there was too much care in all he said,
A hard kind of no-feeling in her touch –

By such rites they saved love's face, and such laws
As prescribe mutual tolerance, charity
To neighbours, strangers, those by nature
Subdued among famines and difficult wars.

# SOLOMON'S MINES

*To Bonamy Dobrée*

Anything to have done!
(The eagle flagged to the sun)
To have discovered and disclosed
The buried thrones, the means used;

Spadework and symbol; each deed
Resurrecting those best dead
Priests, soldiers and kings;
Blazed-out, stripped-out things;

Anything to get up and go
(Let the hewn gates clash to)
Without looking round
Out of that strong land.

# THE DISTANT
# FURY OF BATTLE

Grass resurrects to mask, to strangle,
Words glossed on stone, lopped stone-angel;
But the dead maintain their ground –
That there's no getting round –

Who in places vitally rest,
Named, anonymous; who test
Alike the endurance of yews
Laurels, moonshine, stone, all tissues;

With whom, under licence and duress,
There are pacts made, if not peace.
Union with the stone-wearing dead
Claims the born leader, the prepared

Leader, the devourers and all lean men.
Some, finally, learn to begin.
Some keep to the arrangement of love
(Or similar trust) under whose auspices move

Most subjects, toward the profits of this
Combine of doves and witnesses.
Some, dug out of hot-beds, are brought bare,
Not past conceiving but past care.

# ASMODEUS

I

They, after the slow building of the house,
Furnished it; brought warmth under the skin.
Tiles, that a year's rough wind could rattle loose,
Being close-pressed still kept storms out and storms in.
(Of all primed and vain citadels, to choose
This, to choose this of all times to begin!)
Acknowledging, they said, one who pursues
Hobbies of serious lust and indoor sin,
Clearly they both stood, lovers without fear,
Might toy with fire brought dangerously to hand
To tame, not exorcize, spirits; though the air
Whistled abstracted menace, could confound
Strength by device, by music reaching the ear,
Lightning conducted forcibly to the ground.

## 2

The night, then; bravely stiffen; you are one
Whom stars could burn more deeply than the sun,
Guide-book martyr. You, doubtless, hear wings,
Too sheer for cover, swift; the scattered noise
Of darkness looming with propitious things;
And nests of rumour clustered in the world.
So drummed, so shadowed, your mere trudging voice
Might rave at large while easy truths were told,
Bad perjurable stuff, to be forgiven
Because of this lame journey out of mind.
A tax on men to seventy-times-seven,
A busy vigilance of goose and hound,
Keeps up all guards. Since you are outside, go,
Closing the doors of the house and the head also.

# REQUIEM FOR THE
# PLANTAGENET KINGS

For whom the possessed sea littered, on both shores,
Ruinous arms; being fired, and for good,
To sound the constitution of just wars,
Men, in their eloquent fashion, understood.

Relieved of soul, the dropping-back of dust,
Their usage, pride, admitted within doors;
At home, under caved chantries, set in trust,
With well-dressed alabaster and proved spurs
They lie; they lie; secure in the decay
Of blood, blood-marks, crowns hacked and coveted,
Before the scouring fires of trial-day
Alight on men; before sleeked groin, gored head,
Budge through the clay and gravel, and the sea
Across daubed rock evacuates its dead.

# TWO FORMAL ELEGIES

*For the Jews in Europe*

I

Knowing the dead, and how some are disposed:
Subdued under rubble, water, in sand graves,
In clenched cinders not yielding their abused
Bodies and bonds to those whom war's chance saves
Without the law: we grasp, roughly, the song.
Arrogant acceptance from which song derives
Is bedded with their blood, makes flourish young
Roots in ashes. The wilderness revives,

Deceives with sweetness harshness. Still beneath
Live skin stone breathes, about which fires but play,
Fierce heart that is the iced brain's to command
To judgment – studied reflex, contained breath –
Their best of worlds since, on the ordained day,
This world went spinning from Jehovah's hand.

2

For all that must be gone through, their long death
Documented and safe, we have enough
Witnesses (our world being witness-proof).
The sea flickers, roars, in its wide hearth.
Here, yearly, the pushing midlanders stand
To warm themselves; men, brawny with life,
Women who expect life. They relieve
Their thickening bodies, settle on scraped sand.

Is it good to remind them, on a brief screen,
Of what they have witnessed and not seen?
(Deaths of the city that persistently dies . . . ?)
To put up stones ensures some sacrifice.
Sufficient men confer, carry their weight.
(At whose door does the sacrifice stand or start?)

# METAMORPHOSES

### I THE FEAR

No manner of address will do;
Eloquence is not in that look,
But fear of a furred kind. You
Display the stiff face of shock.

Hate is not in it, nor that
Which has presence, a character
In civil intercourse – deceit
Of a tough weathering-nature.

This fear strikes hard and is gone
And is recognized when found
Not only between dark and dawn,
The summit and the ground.

Through scant pride to be so put out!
But feed, feed, unlyrical scapegoat;
Plague shrines where each fissure blows
Odour of laurel clouding yours.

Exercise, loftily, your visions
Where the mountainous distance
Echoes its unfaltering speech
To mere outcry and harrowing search.

Possessed of agility and passion,
Energy (out-of-town-fashion)
Attack every obstacle
And height; make the sun your pedestal.

Settle all that bad blood;
Be visited, touched, understood;
Be graced, groomed, returned to favour
With admirable restraint and fervour.

And now the sea-scoured temptress, having failed
To scoop out of horizons what birds herald:
Tufts of fresh soil: shakes off an entire sea,
Though not as the dove, harried. Rather, she,

A shark hurricaned to estuary-water,
(The lesser hunter almost by a greater
Devoured) but unflurried, lies, approaches all
Stayers, and searchers of the fanged pool.

Those varied dead. The undiscerning sea
Shelves and dissolves their flesh as it burns spray

Who do not shriek like gulls nor dolphins ride
Crouched under spume to England's erect side

Though there a soaked sleeve lolls or shoe patrols
Tide-padded thick shallows, squats in choked pools

Neither our designed wreaths nor used words
Sink to their melted ears and melted hearts.

5

Doubtless he saw some path clear, having found
His love now fenced him off from the one ground
Where, as he owned, no temperate squalls could move
Either from the profession of their love.

Storm-bound, now she'd outweather him, though he,
Between sun-clouded marshworld and strewn sea
Pitched to extremities, in the rock's vein
Gripped for the winds to roughen and tide stain.

But when he tore his flesh-root and was gone,
Leaving no track, no blood gritting the stone,
Drawn freely to the darkness he had fought
Driven by sulphurous blood and a clenched heart,

Grant the detached, pierced spirit could plunge, soar,
Seeking that love flesh dared not answer for,
Nor suffers now, hammocked in salt tagged cloth
That to be bleached or burned the sea casts out.

# PICTURE OF A NATIVITY

Sea-preserved, heaped with sea-spoils,
Ribs, keels, coral sores,
Detached faces, ephemeral oils,
Discharged on the world's outer shores,

A dumb child-king
Arrives at his right place; rests,
Undisturbed, among slack serpents; beasts
With claws flesh-buttered. In the gathering

Of bestial and common hardship
Artistic men appear to worship
And fall down; to recognize
Familiar tokens; believe their own eyes.

Above the marvel, each rigid head,
Angels, their unnatural wings displayed,
Freeze into an attitude
Recalling the dead.

# CANTICLE
# FOR GOOD FRIDAY

The cross staggered him. At the cliff-top
Thomas, beneath its burden, stood
While the dulled wood
Spat on the stones each drop
Of deliberate blood.

A clamping, cold-figured day
Thomas (not transfigured) stamped, crouched,
Watched
Smelt vinegar and blood. He,
As yet unsearched, unscratched,

And suffered to remain
At such near distance
(A slight miracle might cleanse
His brain
Of all attachments, claw-roots of sense)

In unaccountable darkness moved away,
The strange flesh untouched, carrion-sustenance
Of staunchest love, choicest defiance,
Creation's issue congealing (and one woman's).

# THE GUARDIANS

The young, having risen early, had gone,
Some with excursions beyond the bay-mouth,
Some toward lakes, a fragile reflected sun.
Thunder-heads drift, awkwardly, from the south;

The old watch them. They have watched the safe
Packed harbours topple under sudden gales,
Great tides irrupt, yachts burn at the wharf
That on clean seas pitched their effective sails.

There are silences. These, too, they endure:
Soft comings-on; soft after-shocks of calm.
Quietly they wade the disturbed shore;
Gather the dead as the first dead scrape home.

# THE WHITE SHIP

Where the living with effort go,
Or with expense, the drowned wander
Easily: seaman
And king's son also

Who, by gross error lost,
Drift, now, in salt crushed
Polyp- and mackerel-fleshed
Tides between coast and coast,

Submerge or half-appear.
This does not much matter.
They are put down as dead. Water
Silences all who would interfere;

Retains, still, what it might give
As casually as it took away:
Creatures passed through the wet sieve
Without enrichment or decay.

# WREATHS

1

Each day the tide withdraws; chills us; pastes
The sand with dead gulls, oranges, dead men.
Uttering love, that outlasts or outwastes
Time's attrition, exiles appear again,
But faintly altered in eyes and skin.


2

Into what understanding all have grown!
(Setting aside a few things, the still faces,
Climbing the phosphorus tide, that none will own)
What paradises and watering-places,
What hurts appeased by the sea's handsomeness!

# ELEGIAC STANZAS
## On a Visit to Dove Cottage

*To J. P. Mann*


Mountains, monuments, all forms
Inured to processes and storms
(And they are many); the fashions
Of intercourse between nations:

Customs through which many come
To sink their eyes into a room
Filled with the unused and unworn;
To bite nothings to the bone:

And the daylight between facts;
And the daylight between acts;
Groping of custom towards love;
Past loving, the custom to approve:

A use of words; a rhetoric
As plain as spitting on a stick;
Speech from the ice, the clear-obscure;
The tongue broody in the jaw:

Greatly-aloof, alert, rare
Spirit, conditioned to appear
At the authentic stone or seat:
O near-human spouse and poet,

Mountains, rivers, and grand storms,
Continuous profit, grand customs
(And many of them): O Lakes, Lakes!
O Sentiment upon the rocks!

# AFTER CUMAE

The sun again unearthed, colours come up fresh,
The perennials; and the laurels'
Washable leaves, that seem never to perish,
Obscure the mouthy cave, the dumb grottoes.

From the beginning, in the known world, slide
Drawn echoing hulls, axes grate, and waves
Deposit in their shallow margins varied
Fragments of marine decay and waftage;

And the sometimes-abandoned gods confuse
With immortal essences men's brief lives,
Frequenting the exposed and pious: those
Who stray, as designed, under applied perils,

Whose doom is easy, venturing so far
Without need, other than to freeze or burn,
Their wake, on spread-out oceans, a healed scar
Fingered, themselves the curios of voyage.

# LITTLE APOCALYPSE

## Hölderlin: 1770–1843

Abrupt tempter; close enough to survive
The sun's primitive renewing fury;
Scorched vistas where crawl the injured and brave:
This man stands sealed against their injury:

Hermetic radiance of great suns kept in:
Man's common nature suddenly too rare:
See, for the brilliant coldness of his skin,
The god cast, perfected, among fire.

# THE BIBLIOGRAPHERS

Lucifer blazing in superb effigies
Among the world's ambitious tragedies,
Heaven-sent gift to the dark ages,

Now, in the finest-possible light,
We approach you; can estimate
Your not unnatural height.

Though the discrete progeny,
Out of their swim, go deflated and dry,
We know the feel of you, archaic beauty,

Between the tombs, where the tombs still extrude,
Overshadowing the sun-struck world:
(The shadow-god envisaged in no cloud).

# OF COMMERCE
# AND SOCIETY

## Variations on a Theme

Then hang this picture for a calendar,
As sheep for goat, and pray most fixedly
For the cold martial progress of your star,
With thoughts of commerce and society,
Well-milked Chinese, Negroes who cannot sing,
The Huns gelded and feeding in a ring.
ALLEN TATE: *More Sonnets at Christmas*, 1942

### I THE APOSTLES: VERSAILLES, 1919

They sat. They stood about.
They were estranged. The air,
As water curdles from clear,
Fleshed the silence. They sat.

They were appalled. The bells
In hollowed Europe spilt
To the gods of coin and salt.
The sea creaked with worked vessels.

Europe, the much-scarred, much-scoured terrain,
Its attested liberties, home-produce,
Labelled and looking up, invites use,
Stuffed with artistry and substantial gain:

Shrunken, magnified (nest, holocaust)
Not half innocent and not half undone;
Profiting from custom: its replete strewn
Cities such ample monuments to lost

Nations and generations: its cultural
Or trade skeletons such hand-picked bone:
Flaws in the best, revised science marks down:
Witness many devices; the few natural

Corruptions, graftings; witness classic falls
(The dead subtracted; the greatest resigned);
Witness earth fertilized, decently drained,
The sea decent again behind walls.

i

Slime; the residues of refined tears;
And, salt-bristled, blown on a drying sea,
The sunned and risen faces.

                There's Andromeda
Depicted in relief, after the fashion.

'His guarded eyes under his shielded brow'
Through poisonous baked sea-things Perseus
Goes – clogged sword, clear, aimless mirror –
With nothing to strike at or blind

                in the frothed shallows.

ii

Rivers bring down. The sea
Brings away;
Voids, sucks back, its pearls and auguries.
Eagles or vultures churn the fresh-made skies.

Over the statues, unchanging features
Of commerce and quaint love, soot lies.
Earth steams. The bull and the great mute swan
Strain into life with their notorious cries.

4

Statesmen have known visions. And, not alone,
Artistic men prod dead men from their stone:
Some of us have heard the dead speak:
The dead are my obsession this week

But may be lifted away. In summer
Thunder may strike, or, as a tremor
Of remote adjustment, pass on the far side
From us: however deified and defied

By those it does strike. Many have died. Auschwitz,
Its furnace chambers and lime pits
Half-erased, is half-dead; a fable
Unbelievable in fatted marble.

There is, at times, some need to demonstrate
Jehovah's touchy methods that create
The connoisseur of blood, the smitten man.
At times it seems not common to explain.

Thriving against façades the ignorant sea
Souses our public baths, statues, waste ground:
Archaic earth-shaker, fresh enemy
('The tables of exchange being overturned');

Drowns Babel in upheaval and display;
Unswerving, as were the admired multitudes
Silenced from time to time under its sway.
By all means let us appease the terse gods.

Homage to Henry James

'But then face to face'

Naked, as if for swimming, the martyr
Catches his death in a little flutter
Of plain arrows. A grotesque situation,
But priceless, and harmless to the nation.

Consider such pains 'crystalline': then fine art
Persists where most crystals accumulate.
History can be scraped clean of its old price.
Engrossed in the cold blood of sacrifice

The provident and self-healing gods
Destroy only to save. Well-stocked with foods,
Enlarged and deep-oiled, America
Detects music, apprehends the day-star

Where, sensitive and half-under a cloud,
Europe muddles her dreaming, is loud
And critical beneath the varied domes
Resonant with tribute and with commerce.

# DOCTOR FAUSTUS

For it must needs be that offences come; but woe to
that man by whom the offence cometh.


## 1 THE EMPEROR'S CLOTHES

A way of many ways: a god
Spirals in the pure steam of blood.
And gods – as men – rise from shut tombs
To a disturbance of small drums;

Immaculate plumage of the swan
The common wear. There is no-one
Afraid or overheard, no loud
Voice (though innocently loud).


## 2 THE HARPIES

Having stood hungrily apart
From the gods' politic banquet,
Of all possible false gods
I fall to these gristled shades

That show everything, without lust;
And stumble upon their dead feast
By the torn *Warning To Bathers*
By the torn waters.


## 3 ANOTHER PART OF THE FABLE

The Innocents have not flown;
Too legendary, they laugh;
The lewd uproarious wolf
Brings their house down.

A beast is slain, a beast thrives.
Fat blood squeaks on the sand.
A blinded god believes
That he is not blind.

# A PASTORAL

Mobile, immaculate and austere,
The Pities, their fingers in every wound,
Assess the injured on the obscured frontier;
Cleanse with a kind of artistry the ground
Shared by War. Consultants in new tongues
Prove synonymous our separated wrongs.

We celebrate, fluently and at ease.
Traditional Furies, having thrust, hovered,
Now decently enough sustain Peace.
The unedifying nude dead are soon covered.
Survivors, still given to wandering, find
Their old loves, painted and re-aligned –

Queer, familiar, fostered by superb graft
On treasured foundations, these ideal features.
Men can move with purpose again, or drift,
According to direction. Here are statues
Darkened by laurel; and evergreen names;
Evidently-veiled griefs; impervious tombs.

# ORPHEUS
# AND EURYDICE

Though there are wild dogs
  Infesting the roads
We have recitals, catalogues
  Of protected birds;

And the rare pale sun
  To water our days.
Men turn to savagery now or turn
  To the laws'

Immutable black and red.
  To be judged for his song,
Traversing the still-moist dead,
  The newly-stung,

Love goes, carrying compassion
  To the rawly-difficult;
His countenance, his hands' motion,
  Serene even to a fault.

# IN PIAM MEMORIAM

### 1

Created purely from glass the saint stands,
Exposing his gifted quite empty hands
Like a conjurer about to begin,
A righteous man begging of righteous men.

### 2

In the sun lily-and-gold-coloured,
Filtering the cruder light, he has endured,
A feature for our regard; and will keep;
Of worldly purity the stained archetype.

### 3

The scummed pond twitches. The great holly-tree,
Emptied and shut, blows clear of wasting snow,
The common, puddled substance: beneath,
Like a revealed mineral, a new earth.

# TO THE
# (SUPPOSED) PATRON

Prodigal of loves and barbecues,
Expert in the strangest faunas, at home
He considers the lilies, the rewards.
There is no substitute for a rich man.
At his first entering a new province
With new coin, music, the barest glancing
Of steel or gold suffices. There are many
Tremulous dreams secured under that head.
For his delight and his capacity
To absorb, freshly, the inside-succulence
Of untoughened sacrifice, his bronze agents
Speculate among convertible stones
And drink desert sand. That no mirage
Irritate his mild gaze, the lewd noonday
Is housed in cool places, and fountains
Salt the sparse haze. His flesh is made clean.
For the unfallen – the firstborn, or wise
Councillor – prepared vistas extend
As far as harvest; and idyllic death
Where fish at dawn ignite the powdery lake.

# KING LOG

# OVID IN
# THE THIRD REICH

*non peccat, quaecumque potest peccasse negare,*
*solaque famosam culpa professa facit.*
(AMORES, III, xiv)


I love my work and my children. God
Is distant, difficult. Things happen.
Too near the ancient troughs of blood
Innocence is no earthly weapon.

I have learned one thing: not to look down
So much upon the damned. They, in their sphere,
Harmonize strangely with the divine
Love. I, in mine, celebrate the love-choir.

# ANNUNCIATIONS

I

The Word has been abroad, is back, with a tanned look
From its subsistence in the stiffening-mire.
Cleansing has become killing, the reward
Touchable, overt, clean to the touch.
Now at a distance from the steam of beasts,
The loathly neckings and fat shook spawn
(Each specimen-jar fed with delicate spawn)
The searchers with the curers sit at meat
And are satisfied. Such precious things put down
And the flesh eased through turbulence the soul
Purples itself; each eye squats full and mild
While all who attend to fiddle or to harp
For betterment, flavour their decent mouths
With gobbets of the sweetest sacrifice.

2

O Love, subject of the mere diurnal grind,
Forever being pledged to be redeemed,
Expose yourself for charity; be assured
The body is but husk and excrement.
Enter these deaths according to the law,
O visited women, possessed sons. Foreign lusts
Infringe our restraints; the changeable
Soldiery have their goings-out and comings-in
Dying in abundance. Choicest beasts
Suffuse the gutters with their colourful blood.
Our God scatters corruption. Priests, martyrs,
Parade to this imperious theme: 'O Love,
You know what pains succeed; be vigilant; strive
To recognize the damned among your friends.'

# LOCUST SONGS

*To Allan Seager*


### THE EMBLEM

So with sweet oaths converting the salt earth
To yield, our fathers verged on Paradise:
Each to his own portion of Paradise,
Stung by the innocent venoms of the earth.


### GOOD HUSBANDRY

Out of the foliage of sensual pride
Those teeming apples. Summer burned well
The dramatic flesh; made work for pride
Forking into the tender mouths of Hell

Heaped windfalls, pulp for the Gadarene
Squealers. This must be our reward:
To smell God writhing over the rich scene.
Gluttons for wrath, we stomach our reward.

## SHILOH CHURCH, 1862:
### TWENTY-THREE THOUSAND

O stamping-ground of the shod Word! So hard
On the heels of the damned red-man we came,
Geneva's tribe, outlandish and abhorred –
Bland vistas milky with Jehovah's calm –

Who fell to feasting Nature, the glare
Of buzzards circling; cried to the grim sun
'Jehovah punish us!'; who went too far;
In deserts dropped the odd white turds of bone;

Whose passion was to find out God in this
His natural filth, voyeur of sacrifice, a slow
Bloody unearthing of the God-in-us.
But with what blood, and to what end, Shiloh?

# I HAD HOPE WHEN
# VIOLENCE WAS CEAS'T

Dawnlight freezes against the east-wire.
The guards cough 'raus! 'raus! We flinch and grin,
Our flesh oozing towards its last outrage.
That which is taken from me is not mine.

# SEPTEMBER SONG

*born 19.6.32 – deported 24.9.42*


Undesirable you may have been, untouchable
you were not. Not forgotten
or passed over at the proper time.

As estimated, you died. Things marched,
sufficient, to that end.
Just so much Zyklon and leather, patented
terror, so many routine cries.

(I have made
an elegy for myself it
is true)

September fattens on vines. Roses
flake from the wall. The smoke
of harmless fires drifts to my eyes.

This is plenty. This is more than enough.

# AN ORDER OF SERVICE

He was the surveyor of his own ice-world,
Meticulous at the chosen extreme,
Though what he surveyed may have been nothing.

Let a man sacrifice himself, concede
His mortality and have done with it;
There is no end to that sublime appeal.

In such a light dismiss the unappealing
Blank of his gaze, hopelessly vigilant,
Dazzled by renunciation's glare.

# THE HUMANIST

The *Venice* portrait: he
Broods, the achieved guest
Tired and word-perfect
At the Muses' table.

Virtue is virtù. These
Lips debate and praise
Some rich aphorism,
A delicate white meat.

The commonplace hands once
Thick with Plato's blood
(Tasteless! tasteless!) are laid
Dryly against the robes.

# FUNERAL MUSIC

*William de la Pole, Duke of Suffolk: beheaded 1450*
*John Tiptoft, Earl of Worcester: beheaded 1470*
*Anthony Woodville, Earl Rivers: beheaded 1483*

I

Processionals in the exemplary cave,
Benediction of shadows. Pomfret. London.
The voice fragrant with mannered humility,
With an equable contempt for this world,
'In honorem Trinitatis'. Crash. The head
Struck down into a meaty conduit of blood.
So these dispose themselves to receive each
Pentecostal blow from axe or seraph,
Spattering block-straw with mortal residue.
Psalteries whine through the empyrean. Fire
Flares in the pit, ghosting upon stone
Creatures of such rampant state, vacuous
Ceremony of possession, restless
Habitation, no man's dwelling-place.

2

For whom do we scrape our tribute of pain –
For none but the ritual king? We meditate
A rueful mystery; we are dying
To satisfy fat Caritas, those
Wiped jaws of stone. (Suppose all reconciled
By silent music; imagine the future
Flashed back at us, like steel against sun,
Ultimate recompense.) Recall the cold
Of Towton on Palm Sunday before dawn,
Wakefield, Tewkesbury: fastidious trumpets
Shrilling into the ruck; some trampled
Acres, parched, sodden or blanched by sleet,
Stuck with strange-postured dead. Recall the wind's
Flurrying, darkness over the human mire.

3

They bespoke doomsday and they meant it by
God, their curved metal rimming the low ridge.
But few appearances are like this. Once
Every five hundred years a comet's
Over-riding stillness might reveal men
In such array, livid and featureless,
With England crouched beastwise beneath it all.
'Oh, that old northern business . . .' A field
After battle utters its own sound
Which is like nothing on earth, but is earth.
Blindly the questing snail, vulnerable
Mole emerge, blindly we lie down, blindly
Among carnage the most delicate souls
Tup in their marriage-blood, gasping 'Jesus'.

4

Let mind be more precious than soul; it will not
Endure. Soul grasps its price, begs its own peace,
Settles with tears and sweat, is possibly
Indestructible. That I can believe.
Though I would scorn the mere instinct of faith,
Expediency of assent, if I dared,
What I dare not is a waste history
Or void rule. Averroes, old heathen,
If only you had been right, if Intellect
Itself were absolute law, sufficient grace,
Our lives could be a myth of captivity
Which we might enter: an unpeopled region
Of ever new–fallen snow, a palace blazing
With perpetual silence as with torches.

5

As with torches we go, at wild Christmas,
When we revel in our atonement
Through thirty feasts of unction and slaughter,
What is that but the soul's winter sleep?
So many things rest under consummate
Justice as though trumpets purified law,
Spikenard were the real essence of remorse.
The sky gathers up darkness. When we chant
'Ora, ora pro nobis' it is not
Seraphs who descend to pity but ourselves.
Those righteously-accused those vengeful
Racked on articulate looms indulge us
With lingering shows of pain, a flagrant
Tenderness of the damned for their own flesh:

6

My little son, when you could command marvels
Without mercy, outstare the wearisome
Dragon of sleep, I rejoiced above all –
A stranger well-received in your kingdom.
On those pristine fields I saw humankind
As it was named by the Father; fabulous
Beasts rearing in stillness to be blessed.
The world's real cries reached there, turbulence
From remote storms, rumour of solitudes,
A composed mystery. And so it ends.
Some parch for what they were; others are made
Blind to all but one vision, their necessity
To be reconciled. I believe in my
Abandonment, since it is what I have.

'Prowess, vanity, mutual regard,
It seemed I stared at them, they at me.
That was the gorgon's true and mortal gaze:
Averted conscience turned against itself.'
A hawk and a hawk-shadow. 'At noon,
As the armies met, each mirrored the other;
Neither was outshone. So they flashed and vanished
And all that survived them was the stark ground
Of this pain. I made no sound, but once
I stiffened as though a remote cry
Had heralded my name. It was nothing . . .'
Reddish ice tinged the reeds; dislodged, a few
Feathers drifted across; carrion birds
Strutted upon the armour of the dead.

8

Not as we are but as we must appear,
Contractual ghosts of pity; not as we
Desire life but as they would have us live,
Set apart in timeless colloquy.
So it is required; so we bear witness,
Despite ourselves, to what is beyond us,
Each distant sphere of harmony forever
Poised, unanswerable. If it is without
Consequence when we vaunt and suffer, or
If it is not, all echoes are the same
In such eternity. Then tell me, love,
How that should comfort us – or anyone
Dragged half-unnerved out of this worldly place,
Crying to the end 'I have not finished'.

# FOUR POEMS
# REGARDING THE
# ENDURANCE OF POETS

## MEN ARE A MOCKERY OF ANGELS

*i.m. Tommaso Campanella, priest and poet*

Some days a shadow through
The high window shares my
Prison. I watch a slug
Scale the glinting pit–side
Of its own slime. The cries
As they come are mine; then
God's: my justice, wounds, love,
Derisive light, bread, filth.

To lie here in my strange
Flesh while glutted Torment
Sleeps, stained with its prompt food,
Is a joy past all care
Of the world, for a time.
But we are commanded
To rise, when, in silence,
I would compose my voice.

## A PRAYER TO THE SUN

*i.m. Miguel Hernandez*

i
Darkness
above all things
the Sun
makes
rise

ii
Vultures
salute their meat
at noon
(Hell is
silent)

iii
Blind Sun
our ravager
bless us
so that
we sleep.

## 'DOMAINE PUBLIC'

*i.m. Robert Desnos, died Terezin Camp, 1945*

For reading I can recommend
    the Fathers. How they
cultivate the corrupting flesh:

toothsome contemplation: cleanly
    maggots churning spleen
to milk. For exercise, prolonged

suppression of much improper
    speech from proper tombs.
If the ground opens, should men's mouths

open also? 'I am nothing
    if not saved now!' or
'Christ, what a pantomime!' The days

of the week are seven pits. Look,
    Seigneur, again we
resurrect and the judges come.

*A Valediction to Osip Mandelstam*

Difficult friend, I would have preferred
You to them. The dead keep their sealed lives
And again I am too late. Too late
The salutes, dust-clouds and brazen cries.

Images rear from desolation
Look . . . ruins upon a plain . . .
A few men glare at their hands; others
Grovel for food in the roadside field.

Tragedy has all under regard.
It will not touch us but it is there –
Flawless, insatiate – hard summer sky
Feasting on this, reaching its own end.

# THE IMAGINATIVE LIFE

Evasive souls, of whom the wise lose track,
Die in each night, who, with their day-tongues, sift
The waking-taste of manna or of blood:

The raw magi, part-barbarians,
Entranced by demons and desert frost,
By the irregular visions of a god,

Suffragans of the true seraphs. Lust
Writhes, is dumb savage and in their way
As a virulence natural to the earth.

Renewed glories batten on the poor bones;
Gargantuan mercies whetted by a scent
Of mortal sweat: as though the sleeping flesh

Adored by Furies, stirred, yawned, were driven
In mid-terror to purging and delight.
As though the dead had *Finis* on their brows.

# THE ASSISI FRAGMENTS

*To G. Wilson Knight*

I

Lion and lioness, the mild
Inflammable beasts,
At their precise peril kept
Distance and repose –
And there the serpent
Innocently shone its head.

2

So the hawk had its pursuit. So Death
Opened its childish eyes. So the angels
Overcame Adam: he was defiled
By balm. Creator, and creature made
Of unnatural earth, he howled
To the raven *find me*; to the wolf
*Eat, my brother*; and to the fire *I am clean*.

# HISTORY AS POETRY

Poetry as salutation; taste
Of Pentecost's ashen feast. Blue wounds.
The tongue's atrocities. Poetry
Unearths from among the speechless dead

Lazarus mystified, common man
Of death. The lily rears its gouged face
From the provided loam. Fortunate
Auguries; whirrings; tarred golden dung:

'A resurgence' as they say. The old
Laurels wagging with the new: Selah!
Thus laudable the trodden bone thus
Unanswerable the knack of tongues.

# SOLILOQUIES

### THE STONE MAN

*To Charles Causley*

Recall, now, the omens of childhood:
The nettle-clump and rank elder-tree;
The stones waiting in the mason's yard:

Half-recognized kingdom of the dead:
A deeper landscape lit by distant
Flashings from their journey. At nightfall

My father scuffed clay into the house.
He set his boots on the bleak iron
Of the hearth; ate, drank, unbuckled, slept.

I leaned to the lamp; the pallid moths
Clipped its glass, made an autumnal sound.
Words clawed my mind as though they had smelt

Revelation's flesh . . . So, with an ease
That is dreadful, I summon all back.
The sun bellows over its parched swarms.

What I lost was not a part of this.
The dark-blistered foxgloves, wet berries
Glinting from shadow, small ferns and stones,

Seem fragments, in the observing mind,
Of its ritual power. Old age
Singles them out as though by first-light,

As though a still-life, preserving some
Portion of the soul's feast, went with me
Everywhere, to be hung in strange rooms,

Loneliness being what it is. If
I knew the exact coin for tribute,
Defeat might be bought, processional

Silence gesture its tokens of earth
At my mouth: as in the great death-songs
Of Propertius (although he died young).

# COWAN BRIDGE

## At the site of 'Lowood School'

A lost storm in this temperate place;
The silent direction;
Some ash-trees and foam-patched
Alders at the beck.

All the seasons absorbed
As by a child, safe from rain,
Crouched in the dank
Stench of an elder-bush.

So much that was not justice,
So much that is;
The vulnerable pieties
Not willingly let die;
By chance unmolested
The modesty of her rage.

# FANTASIA ON 'HORBURY'

John Bacchus Dykes, 1859

Dry walls, and nettles battered by the dust,
Odours from gathered water, muddled storm-clouds
Disastrous over the manufactured West Riding.

Mind – a fritter of excrement; step
Aside, step aside, sir! Ah, but a priest
In his prime watches where he goes. He goes

To tender his confession. Forgiveness
Journeys towards him like a brisk traveller
On the same road. Is this Horbury?

Yes: and he will perpetuate this refuge.
Yes: and he will weaken, scribbling, at the end,
Of unspeakable desolation. Really? Good Lord!

Consider him thus animated,
That outworn piety and those plush tunes
Restored for the sake of a paradox

And the too-fashionable North. Or, again,
Consider him catspawed by an indolent poem,
This place not of his choosing, this menace

From concave stormlight a freak suggestion . . .
These heads of nettles lopped into the dust . . .

# THREE BAROQUE
# MEDITATIONS

I

Do words make up the majesty
Of man, and his justice
Between the stones and the void?

How they watch us, the demons
Plugging their dumb wounds! When
Exorcized they shrivel yet thrive.

An owl plunges to its tryst
With a field-mouse in the sharp night.
My fire squeals and lies still.

Minerva, receive this hard
Praise: I speak well of Death;
I confess to the priest in me;

I am shadowed by the wise bird
Of necessity, the lithe
Paradigm Sleep-and-Kill.

Anguish bloated by the replete scream.
Flesh of abnegation: the poem
Moves grudgingly to its extreme form,

Vulnerable, to the lamp's fierce head
Of well-trimmed light. In darkness outside,
Foxes and rain-sleeked stones and the dead –

Aliens of such a theme – endure
Until I could cry 'Death! Death!' as though
To exacerbate that suave power;

But refrain. For I am circumspect,
Lifting the spicy lid of my tact
To sniff at the myrrh. It is perfect

In its impalpable bitterness,
Scent of a further country where worse
Furies promenade and bask their claws.

So white I was, he would have me cry
  'Unclean!' murderously
To heal me with far-fetched blood.

I writhed to conceive of him.
I clawed to becalm him.
Some nights, I witnessed his face in sleep

And dreamed of my father's
House. (By day he professed languages –
  Disciplines of languages)

By day I cleansed my thin tongue
From its nightly prowl, its vixen-skill,
  His sacramental mouth

  That justified my flesh
And moved well among women
In nuances and imperatives.

This was the poet of a people's
  Love. I hated him. He weeps,
Solemnizing his loss.

# THE SONGBOOK
# OF SEBASTIAN ARRURRUZ

## Sebastian Arrurruz: 1868–1922

I

Ten years without you. For so it happens.
Days make their steady progress, a routine
That is merciful and attracts nobody.

Already, like a disciplined scholar,
I piece fragments together, past conjecture
Establishing true sequences of pain;

For so it is proper to find value
In a bleak skill, as in the thing restored:
The long-lost words of choice and valediction.

### i

'One cannot lose what one has not possessed.'
So much for that abrasive gem.
I can lose what I want. I want you.

### ii

Oh my dear one, I shall grieve for you
For the rest of my life with slightly
Varying cadence, oh my dear one.

### iii

Half-mocking the half-truth, I note
'The wild brevity of sensual love'.
I am shaken, even by that.

### iv

It is to him I write, it is to her
I speak in contained silence. Will they be touched
By the unfamiliar passion between them?

3

What other men do with other women
Is for me neither orgy nor sacrament
Nor a language of foreign candour

But is mere occasion or chance distance
Out of which you might move and speak my name
As I speak yours, bargaining with sleep's

Miscellaneous gods for as much
As I can have: an alien landscape,
The dream where you are always to be found.

4

A workable fancy. Old petulant
Sorrow comes back to us, metamorphosed
And semi-precious. Fortuitous amber.
As though this recompensed our deprivation.
See how each fragment kindles as we turn it,
At the end, into the light of appraisal.

5

Love, oh my love, it will come
Sure enough. A storm
Broods over the dry earth all day.
At night the shutters throb in its downpour.

The metaphor holds; is a snug house.
You are outside, lost somewhere. I find myself
Devouring verses of stranger passion
And exile. The exact words

Are fed into my blank hunger for you.

## POSTURES

I imagine, as I imagine us
Each time more stylized more lovingly
Detailed, that I am not myself
But someone I might have been: sexless,
Indulgent about art, relishing
Let us say the well-schooled
Postures of *St Anthony* or *St Jerome*,
Those peaceful hermaphrodite dreams
Through which the excess of memory
Pursues its own abstinence.

## FROM THE LATIN

There would have been things to say, quietness
That could feed on our lust, refreshed
Trivia, the occurrences of the day;
And at night my tongue in your furrow.

Without you I am mocked by courtesies
And chat, where satisfied women push
Dutifully toward some unneeded guest
Desirable features of conversation.

So, remotely, in your part of the world:
the ripe glandular blooms, and cypresses
shivering with heat (which we have borne
also, in our proper ways) I turn my mind
towards delicate pillage, the provenance
of shards glazed and unglazed, the three
kinds of surviving grain. I hesitate amid
circumstantial disasters. I gaze at the
authentic dead.

## A SONG FROM ARMENIA

Roughly-silvered leaves that are the snow
On Ararat seen through those leaves.
The sun lays down a foliage of shade.

A drinking-fountain pulses its head
Two or three inches from the troughed stone.
An old woman sucks there, gripping the rim.

Why do I have to relive, even now,
Your mouth, and your hand running over me
Deft as a lizard, like a sinew of water?

## TO HIS WIFE

You ventured occasionally –
As though this were another's house –
Not intimate but an acquaintance
Flaunting her modest claim; like one
Idly commiserated by new-mated
Lovers rampant in proper delight
When all their guests have gone.

11

Scarcely speaking: it becomes as a
Coolness between neighbours. Often
There is this orgy of sleep. I wake
To caress propriety with odd words
And enjoy abstinence in a vocation
Of now-almost-meaningless despair.

# MERCIAN HYMNS

# I

King of the perennial holly-groves, the riven sand-stone: overlord of the M5: architect of the historic rampart and ditch, the citadel at Tamworth, the summer hermitage in Holy Cross: guardian of the Welsh Bridge and the Iron Bridge: contractor to the desirable new estates: saltmaster: money-changer: commissioner for oaths: martyrologist: the friend of Charlemagne.

'I liked that,' said Offa, 'sing it again.'

## II

A pet-name, a common name. Best-selling brand, curt
   graffito. A laugh; a cough. A syndicate. A specious
   gift. Scoffed-at horned phonograph.

The starting-cry of a race. A name to conjure with.

# III

On the morning of the crowning we chorused our re-
mission from school. It was like Easter: hankies
and gift-mugs approved by his foreign gaze, the
village-lintels curlered with paper flags.

We gaped at the car-park of 'The Stag's Head' where a
bonfire of beer-crates and holly-boughs whistled
above the tar. And the chef stood there, a king in
his new-risen hat, sealing his brisk largesse with
'any mustard?'

# IV

I was invested in mother-earth, the crypt of roots
and endings. Child's-play. I abode there, bided my
time: where the mole

shouldered the clogged wheel, his gold solidus; where
dry-dust badgers thronged the Roman flues, the
long-unlooked-for mansions of our tribe.

# V

So much for the elves' wergild, the true governance
    of England, the gaunt warrior-gospel armoured in
    engraved stone. I wormed my way heavenward for
    ages amid barbaric ivy, scrollwork of fern.

Exile or pilgrim set me once more upon that ground:
    my rich and desolate childhood. Dreamy, smug-faced,
    sick on outings – I who was taken to be a king of
    some kind, a prodigy, a maimed one.

# VI

The princes of Mercia were badger and raven. Thrall
to their freedom, I dug and hoarded. Orchards
fruited above clefts. I drank from honeycombs of
chill sandstone.

'A boy at odds in the house, lonely among brothers.'
But I, who had none, fostered a strangeness; gave
myself to unattainable toys.

Candles of gnarled resin, apple-branches, the tacky
mistletoe. 'Look' they said and again 'look.' But
I ran slowly; the landscape flowed away, back to
its source.

In the schoolyard, in the cloakrooms, the children
boasted their scars of dried snot; wrists and
knees garnished with impetigo.

# VII

Gasholders, russet among fields. Milldams, marlpools that lay unstirring. Eel-swarms. Coagulations of frogs: once, with branches and half-bricks, he battered a ditchful; then sidled away from the stillness and silence.

Ceolred was his friend and remained so, even after the day of the lost fighter: a biplane, already obsolete and irreplaceable, two inches of heavy snub silver. Ceolred let it spin through a hole in the classroom-floorboards, softly, into the rat-droppings and coins.

After school he lured Ceolred, who was sniggering with fright, down to the old quarries, and flayed him. Then, leaving Ceolred, he journeyed for hours, calm and alone, in his private derelict sandlorry named *Albion*.

# VIII

The mad are predators. Too often lately they harbour
   against us. A novel heresy exculpates all maimed
   souls. Abjure it! I am the King of Mercia, and
   I know.

Threatened by phone-calls at midnight, venomous let-
   ters, forewarned I have thwarted their imminent
   devices.

Today I name them; tomorrow I shall express the new
   law. I dedicate my awakening to this matter.

# IX

The strange church smelled a bit 'high', of censers
and polish. The strange curate was just as ap-
propriate: he took off into the marriage-service.
No-one cared to challenge that gambit.

Then he dismissed you, and the rest of us followed,
sheepish next-of-kin, to the place without the
walls: spoil-heaps of chrysanths dead in their
plastic macs, eldorado of washstand-marble.

Embarrassed, we dismissed ourselves: the three mute
great-aunts borne away down St Chad's Garth in
a stiff-backed Edwardian Rolls.

I unburden the saga of your burial, my dear. You had
lived long enough to see things 'nicely settled'.

# X

He adored the desk, its brown-oak inlaid with ebony,
assorted prize pens, the seals of gold and base
metal into which he had sunk his name.

It was there that he drew upon grievances from the
people; attended to signatures and retributions;
forgave the death-howls of his rival. And there
he exchanged gifts with the Muse of History.

What should a man make of remorse, that it might
profit his soul? Tell me. Tell everything to
Mother, darling, and God bless.

He swayed in sunlight, in mild dreams. He tested the
little pears. He smeared catmint on his palm for
his cat Smut to lick. He wept, attempting to mas-
ter *ancilla* and *servus*.

Coins handsome as Nero's; of good substance and
weight. *Offa Rex* resonant in silver, and the
names of his moneyers. They struck with account-
able tact. They could alter the king's face.

Exactness of design was to deter imitation; muti-
lation if that failed. Exemplary metal, ripe for
commerce. Value from a sparse people, scrapers of
salt-pans and byres.

Swathed bodies in the long ditch; one eye upstaring.
It is safe to presume, here, the king's anger. He
reigned forty years. Seasons touched and retouched
the soil.

Heathland, new-made watermeadow. Charlock, marsh-
marigold. Crepitant oak forest where the boar
furrowed black mould, his snout intimate with
worms and leaves.

# XII

Their spades grafted through the variably-resistant soil. They clove to the hoard. They ransacked epiphanies, vertebrae of the chimera, armour of wild bees' larvae. They struck the fire-dragon's faceted skin.

The men were paid to caulk water-pipes. They brewed and pissed amid splendour; their latrine seethed its estuary through nettles. They are scattered to your collations, moldywarp.

It is autumn. Chestnut-boughs clash their inflamed leaves. The garden festers for attention: telluric cultures enriched with shards, corms, nodules, the sunk solids of gravity. I have raked up a golden and stinking blaze.

# XIII

Trim the lamp; polish the lens; draw, one by one, rare
coins to the light. Ringed by its own lustre, the
masterful head emerges, kempt and jutting, out of
England's well. Far from his underkingdom of crin-
oid and crayfish, the rune-stone's province, *Rex
Totius Anglorum Patriae*, coiffured and ageless,
portrays the self-possession of his possession,
cushioned on a legend.

# XIV

Dismissing reports and men, he put pressure on the
wax, blistered it to a crest. He threatened mal-
efactors with ash from his noon cigar.

When the sky cleared above Malvern, he lingered in
his orchard; by the quiet hammer-pond. Trout-fry
simmered there, translucent, as though forming the
water's underskin. He had a care for natural min-
utiae. What his gaze touched was his tenderness.
Woodlice sat pellet-like in the cracked bark and
a snail sugared its new stone.

At dinner, he relished the mockery of drinking his
family's health. He did this whenever it suited
him, which was not often.

# XV

Tutting, he wrenched at a snarled root of dead crab-
apple. It rose against him. In brief cavort he was
Cernunnos, the branched god, lightly concussed.

He divided his realm. It lay there like a dream. An
ancient land, full of strategy. Ramparts of com-
post pioneered by red-helmeted worms. Hemlock in
ambush, night-soil, tetanus. A wasps' nest en-
sconced in the hedge-bank, a reliquary or wrapped
head, the corpse of Cernunnos pitching dayward
its feral horns.

# XVI

Clash of salutation. As keels thrust into shingle.
Ambassadors, pilgrims. What is carried over? The
Frankish gift, two-edged, regaled with slaughter.

The sword is in the king's hands; the crux a crafts-
man's triumph. Metal effusing its own fragrance,
a variety of balm. And other miracles, other
exchanges.

Shafts from the winter sun homing upon earth's rim.
Christ's mass: in the thick of a snowy forest the
flickering evergreen fissured with light.

Attributes assumed, retribution entertained. What is
borne amongst them? Too much or too little. In-
dulgences of bartered acclaim; an expenditure, a
hissing. Wine, urine and ashes.

# XVII

He drove at evening through the hushed Vosges. The
car radio, glimmering, received broken utterance
from the horizon of storms . . .

'God's honour – our bikes touched; he skidded and came
off.' 'Liar.' A timid father's protective bellow.
Disfigurement of a village-king. 'Just look at
the bugger . . .'

His maroon GT chanted then overtook. He lavished on
the high valleys its *haleine*.

# XVIII

At Pavia, a visitation of some sorrow. Boethius'
dungeon. He shut his eyes, gave rise to a tower
out of the earth. He willed the instruments of
violence to break upon meditation. Iron buckles
gagged; flesh leaked rennet over them; the men
stooped, disentangled the body.

He wiped his lips and hands. He strolled back to the
car, with discreet souvenirs for consolation and
philosophy. He set in motion the furtherance of
his journey. To watch the Tiber foaming out
much blood.

# XIX

Behind the thorn-trees thin smoke, scutch-grass or
    wattle smouldering. At this distance it is hard
    to tell. Far cries impinge like the faint tink-
    ing of iron.

We have a kitchen-garden riddled with toy-shards,
    with splinters of habitation. The children shriek
    and scavenge, play havoc. They incinerate boxes,
    rags and old tyres. They haul a sodden log, hung
    with soft shields of fungus, and launch it upon
    the flames.

# XX

Primeval heathland spattered with the bones of mice
and birds; where adders basked and bees made pro-
vision, mantling the inner walls of their burh:

Coiled entrenched England: brickwork and paintwork
stalwart above hacked marl. The clashing primary
colours – 'Ethandune', Catraeth', 'Maldon', 'Pen-
gwern'. Steel against yew and privet. Fresh
dynasties of smiths.

# XXI

Cohorts of charabancs fanfared Offa's province and
his concern, negotiating the by-ways from Teme
to Trent. Their windshields dripped butterflies.
Stranded on hilltops they signalled with plumes
of steam. Twilight menaced the land. The young
women wept and surrendered.

Still, everyone was cheerful, heedless in such days:
at summer weekends dipping into valleys beyond
Mercia's dyke. Tea was enjoyed, by lakesides where
all might fancy carillons of real Camelot vi-
brating through the silent water.

Gradually, during the years, deciduous velvet peeled
from evergreen albums and during the years more
treasures were mislaid: the harp-shaped brooches,
the nuggets of fool's gold.

# XXII

We ran across the meadow scabbed with cow-dung, past
the crab-apple trees and camouflaged nissen hut.
It was curfew-time for our war-band.

At home the curtains were drawn. The wireless boomed
its commands. I loved the battle-anthems and the
gregarious news.

Then, in the earthy shelter, warmed by a blue-glassed
storm-lantern, I huddled with stories of dragon-
tailed airships and warriors who took wing im-
mortal as phantoms.

# XXIII

In tapestries, in dreams, they gathered, as it was en-
acted, the return, the re-entry of transcendence
into this sublunary world. *Opus Anglicanum*, their
stringent mystery riddled by needles: the silver
veining, the gold leaf, voluted grape-vine, master-
works of treacherous thread.

They trudged out of the dark, scraping their boots
free from lime-splodges and phlegm. They munched
cold bacon. The lamps grew plump with oily re-
liable light.

Itinerant through numerous domains, of his lord's
    retinue, to Compostela. Then home for a lifetime
    amid West Mercia this master-mason as I envisage
    him, intent to pester upon tympanum and chancel-
    arch his moody testament, confusing warrior with
    lion, dragon-coils, tendrils of the stony vine.

Where best to stand? Easter sunrays catch the ob-
    lique face of Adam scrumping through leaves; pale
    spree of evangelists and, there, a cross Christ
    mumming child Adam out of Hell

('Et exspecto resurrectionem mortuorum' dust in the
    eyes, on clawing wings, and lips)

Brooding on the eightieth letter of *Fors Clavigera*,
    I speak this in memory of my grandmother, whose
    childhood and prime womanhood were spent in the
    nailer's darg.

The nailshop stood back of the cottage, by the fold.
    It reeked stale mineral sweat. Sparks had furred
    its low roof. In dawn-light the troughed water
    floated a damson-bloom of dust –

not to be shaken by posthumous clamour. It is one
    thing to celebrate the 'quick forge', another
    to cradle a face hare-lipped by the searing wire.

Brooding on the eightieth letter of *Fors Clavigera*,
    I speak this in memory of my grandmother, whose
    childhood and prime womanhood were spent in the
    nailer's darg.

## XXVI

Fortified in their front parlours, at Yuletide men
   are the more murderous. Drunk, they defy battle-
   axes, bellow of whale-bone and dung.

Troll-wives, groaners in sweetness, tooth-bewitchers,
   you too must purge for the surfeit of England –
   who have scattered peppermint and confetti, your
   hundreds-and-thousands.

'Now when King Offa was alive and dead', they were
    all there, the funereal gleemen: papal legate and
    rural dean; Merovingian car-dealers, Welsh mercen-
    aries; a shuffle of house-carls.

He was defunct. They were perfunctory. The ceremony
    stood acclaimed. The mob received memorial vouch-
    ers and signs.

After that shadowy, thrashing midsummer hail-storm,
    Earth lay for a while, the ghost-bride of livid
    Thor, butcher of strawberries, and the shire-tree
    dripped red in the arena of its uprooting.

# XXVIII

Processes of generation; deeds of settlement. The
urge to marry well; wit to invest in the proper-
ties of healing-springs. Our children and our
children's children, o my masters.

Tracks of ancient occupation. Frail ironworks rust-
ing in the thorn-thicket. Hearthstones; charred
lullabies. A solitary axe-blow that is the echo
of a lost sound.

Tumult recedes as though into the long rain. Groves
of legendary holly; silverdark the ridged gleam.

'Not strangeness, but strange likeness. Obstinate, outclassed forefathers, I too concede, I am your staggeringly-gifted child.'

So, murmurous, he withdrew from them. Gran lit the gas, his dice whirred in the ludo-cup, he entered into the last dream of Offa the King.

## XXX

And it seemed, while we waited, he began to walk to-
    wards us            he vanished

he left behind coins, for his lodging, and traces of
    red mud.

# TENEBRAE

# THE PENTECOST CASTLE

It is terrible to desire and not
possess, and terrible to possess
and not desire.

W. B. YEATS

What we love in other human
beings is the hoped-for satisfaction
of our desire. We do not love their
desire. If what we loved in them
was their desire, then we should
love them as ourself.

SIMONE WEIL


I


They slew by night
upon the road
Medina's pride
Olmedo's flower

shadows warned him
not to go
not to go
along that road

weep for your lord
Medina's pride
Olmedo's flower
there in the road

2

Down in the orchard
I met my death
under the briar rose
I lie slain

I was going
to gather flowers
my love waited
among the trees

down in the orchard
I met my death
under the briar rose
I lie slain


3

You watchers on the wall
grown old with care
I too looked from the wall
I shall look no more

tell us what you saw
the lord I sought to serve
caught in the thorn grove
his blood on his brow

you keepers of the wall
what friend or enemy
sets free the cry
of the bell

4

At dawn the Mass
burgeons from stone
a Jesse tree
of resurrection

budding with candle
flames the gold
and the white wafers
of the feast

and ghosts for love
void a few tears
of wax upon
forlorn altars


5

Goldfinch and hawk
and the grey aspen tree
I have run to the river
mother call me home

the leaves glint in the wind
turning their quiet song
the wings flash and are still
I sleep in the shade

when I cried out you
made no reply
tonight I shall pass by
without a sound

## 6

Slowly my heron flies
pierced by the blade
mounting in slow pain
strikes the air with its cries

goes seeking the high rocks
where no man can climb
where the wild balsam stirs
by the little stream

the rocks the high rocks
are brimming with flowers
there love grows and there love
rests and is saved


## 7

I went out early
to the far field
ermine and lily
and yet a child

Love stood before me
in that place
prayers could not lure me
to Christ's house

Christ the deceiver
took all I had
his darkness ever
my fair reward

## 8

And you my spent heart's treasure
my yet unspent desire
measurer past all measure
cold paradox of fire

as seeker so forsaken
consentingly denied
your solitude a token
the sentries at your side

fulfilment to my sorrow
indulgence of your prey
the sparrowhawk the sparrow
the nothing that you say


## 9

This love will see me dead
he has the place in mind
where I am free to die
be true at last true love

my love meet me half-way
I bear no sword of fear
where you dwell I
dwell also says my lord

dealing his five wounds
so cunning and so true
of love to rouse this death
I die to sleep in love

10

St James and St John
bless the road she has gone
St John and St James
a rosary of names

child-beads of fingered bread
never-depleted heart's food
the nominal the real
subsistence past recall

bread we shall never break
love-runes we cannot speak
scrolled effigy of a cry
our passion its display

11

If the night is dark
and the way short
why do you hold back
dearest heart

though I may never
see you again
touch me I will shiver
at the unseen

the night is so dark
the way so short
why do you not break
o my heart

## 12

Married and not for love
you of all women
you of all women
my soul's darling my love

faithful to my desire
lost in the dream's grasp where
shall I find you everywhere
unmatched in my desire

each of us dispossessed
so richly in my sleep
I rise out of my sleep
crying like one possessed


## 13

Splendidly-shining darkness
proud citadel of meekness
likening us our unlikeness
majesty of our distress

emptiness ever thronging
untenable belonging
how long until this longing
end in unending song

and soul for soul discover
no strangeness to dissever
and lover keep with lover
a moment and for ever

14

As he is wounded
I am hurt
he bleeds from pride
I from my heart

as he is dying
I shall live
in grief desiring
still to grieve

as he is living
I shall die
sick of forgiving
such honesty


15

I shall go down
to the lovers' well
and wash this wound
that will not heal

beloved soul
what shall you see
nothing at all
yet eye to eye

depths of non-being
perhaps too clear
my desire dying
as I desire

# LACHRIMAE
## or
## Seven tears figured in seven passionate Pavans

Passions I allow, and loves I approve, onely
I would wishe that men would alter their
object and better their intent.
ST ROBERT SOUTHWELL, *Marie Magdalens Funeral Teares*, 1591.


### I  LACHRIMAE VERAE

Crucified Lord, you swim upon your cross
and never move. Sometimes in dreams of hell
the body moves but moves to no avail
and is at one with that eternal loss.

You are the castaway of drowned remorse,
you are the world's atonement on the hill.
This is your body twisted by our skill
into a patience proper for redress.

I cannot turn aside from what I do;
you cannot turn away from what I am.
You do not dwell in me nor I in you

however much I pander to your name
or answer to your lords of revenue,
surrendering the joys that they condemn.

Splendour of life so splendidly contained,
brilliance made bearable. It is the east
light's embodiment, fit to be caressed,
the god Amor with his eyes of diamond,

celestial worldliness on which has dawned
intelligence of angels, Midas' feast,
the stony hunger of the dispossessed
locked into Eden by their own demand.

Self-love, the slavish master of this trade,
conquistador of fashion and remark,
models new heavens in his masquerade,

its images intense with starry work,
until he tires and all that he has made
vanishes in the chaos of the dark.

The Jesus-faced man walking crowned with flies
who swats the roadside grass or glances up
at the streaked gibbet with its birds that swoop,
who scans his breviary while the sweat dries,

fades, now, among the fading tapestries,
brooches of crimson tears where no eyes weep,
a mouth unstitched into a rimless cup,
torn clouds the cauldrons of the martyrs' cries.

Clamorous love, its faint and baffled shout,
its grief that would betray him to our fear,
he suffers for our sake, or does not hear

above the hiss of shadows on the wheat.
Viaticum transfigures earth's desire
in rising vernicles of summer air.

Crucified Lord, however much I burn
to be enamoured of your paradise,
knowing what ceases and what will not cease,
frightened of hell, not knowing where to turn,

I fall between harsh grace and hurtful scorn.
You are the crucified who crucifies,
self-withdrawn even from your own device,
your trim-plugged body, wreath of rakish thorn.

What grips me then, or what does my soul grasp?
If I grasp nothing what is there to break?
You are beyond me, innermost true light,

uttermost exile for no exile's sake,
king of our earth not caring to unclasp
its void embrace, the semblance of your quiet.

Loves I allow and passions I approve:
Ash-Wednesday feasts, ascetic opulence,
the wincing lute, so real in its pretence,
itself a passion amorous of love.

Self-wounding martyrdom, what joys you have,
true-torn among this fictive consonance,
music's creation of the moveless dance,
the decreation to which all must move.

Self-seeking hunter of forms, there is no end
to such pursuits. None can revoke your cry.
Your silence is an ecstasy of sound

and your nocturnals blaze upon the day.
I founder in desire for things unfound.
I stay amid the things that will not stay.

Crucified Lord, so naked to the world,
you live unseen within that nakedness,
consigned by proxy to the judas-kiss
of our devotion, bowed beneath the gold,

with re-enactments, penances foretold:
scentings of love across a wilderness
of retrospection, wild and objectless
longings incarnate in the carnal child.

Beautiful for themselves the icons fade;
the lions and the hermits disappear.
Triumphalism feasts on empty dread,

fulfilling triumphs of the festal year.
We find you wounded by the token spear.
Dominion is swallowed with your blood.

What is there in my heart that you should sue
so fiercely for its love? What kind of care
brings you as though a stranger to my door
through the long night and in the icy dew

seeking the heart that will not harbour you,
that keeps itself religiously secure?
At this dark solstice filled with frost and fire
your passion's ancient wounds must bleed anew.

So many nights the angel of my house
has fed such urgent comfort through a dream,
whispered 'your lord is coming, he is close'

that I have drowsed half-faithful for a time
bathed in pure tones of promise and remorse:
'tomorrow I shall wake to welcome him.'

# AN APOLOGY FOR THE REVIVAL OF CHRISTIAN ARCHITECTURE IN ENGLAND

the spiritual, Platonic old England . . .
S. T. COLERIDGE, *Anima Poetae*

'Your situation', said Coningsby, looking up the green
and silent valley, 'is absolutely poetic.'
'I try sometimes to fancy', said Mr Millbank, with a
rather fierce smile, 'that I am in the New World.'
BENJAMIN DISRAELI, *Coningsby*


I  QUAINT MAZES

And, after all, it is to them we return.
Their triumph is to rise and be our hosts:
lords of unquiet or of quiet sojourn,
those muddy-hued and midge-tormented ghosts.

On blustery lilac-bush and terrace-urn
bedaubed with bloom Linnaean pentecosts
put their pronged light; the chilly fountains burn.
Religion of the heart, with trysts and quests

and pangs of consolation, its hawk's hood
twitched off for sweet carnality, again
rejoices in old hymns of servitude,

haunting the sacred well, the hidden shrine.
It is the ravage of the heron wood;
it is the rood blazing upon the green.

November rips gold foil from the oak ridges.
Dour folk huddle in High Hoyland, Penistone.
The tributaries of the Sheaf and Don
bulge their dull spate, cramming the poor bridges.

The North Sea batters our shepherds' cottages
from sixty miles. No sooner has the sun
swung clear above earth's rim than it is gone.
We live like gleaners of its vestiges

knowing we flourish, though each year a child
with the set face of a tomb-weeper is put down
for ever and ever. Why does the air grow cold

in the region of mirrors? And who is this clown
doffing his mask at the masked threshold
to selfless raptures that are all his own?

## 3 WHO ARE THESE COMING TO THE SACRIFICE?

High voices in domestic chapels; praise;
praise-worthy feuds; new-burgeoned spires that sprung
crisp-leaved as though from dropping-wells. The young
ferns root among our vitrified tears.

What an elopement that was: the hired chaise
tore through the fir-grove, scattered kinsmen flung
buckshot and bridles, and the tocsin swung
from the tarred bellcote dappled with dove-smears.

Wires tarnish in gilt corridors, in each room
stiff with the bric-a-brac of loss and gain.
Love fled, truly outwitted, through a swirl

of long-laid dust. Today you sip and smile
though still not quite yourself. Guarding its pane
the spider looms against another storm.

Make miniatures of the once-monstrous theme:
the red–coat devotees, mêlées of wheels,
Jagannath's lovers. With indifferent aim
unleash the rutting cannon at the walls

of forts and palaces; pollute the wells.
Impound the memoirs for their bankrupt shame,
fantasies of true destiny that kills
'under the sanction of the English name'.

Be moved by faith, obedience without fault,
the flawless hubris of heroic guilt,
the grace of visitation; and be stirred

by all her god-quests, her idolatries,
in conclave of abiding injuries,
sated upon the stillness of the bride.

Suppose they sweltered here three thousand years
patient for our destruction. There is a greeting
beyond the act. Destiny is the great thing,
true lord of annexation and arrears.

Our law-books overrule the emperors.
The mango is the bride-bed of light. Spring
jostles the flame-tree. But new mandates bring
new images of faith, good subahdars!

The flittering candles of the wayside shrines
melt into dawn. The sun surmounts the dust.
Krishna from Radha lovingly untwines.

Lugging the earth, the oxen bow their heads.
The alien conscience of our days is lost
among the ruins and on endless roads.

Malcolm and Frere, Colebrooke and Elphinstone,
the life of empire like the life of the mind
'simple, sensuous, passionate', attuned
to the clear theme of justice and order, gone.

Gone the ascetic pastimes, the Persian
scholarship, the wild boar run to ground,
the watercolours of the sun and wind.
Names rise like outcrops on the rich terrain,

like carapaces of the Mughal tombs
lop-sided in the rice-fields, boarded-up
near railway-crossings and small aerodromes.

'India's a peacock-shrine next to a shop
selling mangola, sitars, lucky charms,
heavenly Buddhas smiling in their sleep.'

Pitched high above the shallows of the sea
lone bells in gritty belfries do not ring
but coil a far and inward echoing
out of the air that thrums. Enduringly,

fuchsia-hedges fend between cliff and sky;
brown stumps of headstones tamp into the ling
the ruined and the ruinously strong.
Platonic England grasps its tenantry

where wild-eyed poppies raddle tawny farms
and wild swans root in lily-clouded lakes.
Vulnerable to each other the twin forms

of sleep and waking touch the man who wakes
to sudden light, who thinks that this becalms
even the phantoms of untold mistakes.

While friends defected, you stayed and were sure,
fervent in reason, watchful of each name:
a signet-seal's unostentatious gem
gleams against walnut on the escritoire,

focus of reckoning and judicious prayer.
This is the durable covenant, a room
quietly furnished with stuff of martyrdom,
lit by the flowers and moths from your own shire,

by silvery vistas frothed with convolvulus,
radiance of dreams hardly to be denied.
The twittering pipistrelle, so strange and close,

plucks its curt flight through the moist eventide;
the children thread among old avenues
of snowberries, clear-calling as they fade.

Autumn resumes the land, ruffles the woods
with smoky wings, entangles them. Trees shine
out from their leaves, rocks mildew to moss-green;
the avenues are spread with brittle floods.

Platonic England, house of solitudes,
rests in its laurels and its injured stone,
replete with complex fortunes that are gone,
beset by dynasties of moods and clouds.

It stands, as though at ease with its own world,
the mannerly extortions, languid praise,
all that devotion long since bought and sold,

the rooms of cedar and soft-thudding baize,
tremulous boudoirs where the crystals kissed
in cabinets of amethyst and frost.

Remember how, at seven years, the decrees
were brought home: child-soul must register
for Christ's dole, be allotted its first Easter,
blanch-white and empty, chilled by the lilies,

betrothed among the well-wishers and spies.
Reverend Mother, breakfastless, could feast her
constraint on terracotta and alabaster
and brimstone and the sweets of paradise.

Theology makes good bedside reading. Some
who are lost covet scholastic proof,
subsistence of probation, modest balm.

The wooden wings of justice borne aloof,
we close our eyes to Anselm and lie calm.
All night the cisterns whisper in the roof.

The pigeon purrs in the wood; the wood has gone;
dark leaves that flick to silver in the gust,
and the marsh-orchids and the heron's nest,
goldgrimy shafts and pillars of the sun.

Weightless magnificence upholds the past.
Cement recesses smell of fur and bone
and berries wrinkle in the badger-run
and wiry heath-fern scatters its fresh rust.

'O clap your hands' so that the dove takes flight,
bursts through the leaves with an untidy sound,
plunges its wings into the green twilight

above this long-sought and forsaken ground,
the half-built ruins of the new estate,
warheads of mushrooms round the filter-pond.

Stroke the small silk with your whispering hands,
godmother; nod and nod from the half-gloom;
broochlight intermittent between the fronds,
the owl immortal in its crystal dome.

Along the mantelpiece veined lustres trill,
the clock discounts us with a telling chime.
Familiar ministrants, clerks-of-appeal,
burnish upon the threshold of the dream:

churchwardens in wing-collars bearing scrolls
of copyhold well-tinctured and well-tied.
Your photo-albums loved by the boy-king

preserve in sepia waterglass the souls
of distant cousins, virgin till they died,
and the lost delicate suitors who could sing.

So to celebrate that kingdom: it grows
greener in winter, essence of the year;
the apple-branches musty with green fur.
In the viridian darkness of its yews

it is an enclave of perpetual vows
broken in time. Its truth shows disrepair,
disfigured shrines, their stones of gossamer,
Old Moore's astrology, all hallows,

the squire's effigy bewigged with frost,
and hobnails cracking puddles before dawn.
In grange and cottage girls rise from their beds

by candlelight and mend their ruined braids.
Touched by the cry of the iconoclast,
how the rose-window blossoms with the sun!

# TWO CHORALE-PRELUDES
## on melodies by Paul Celan

### I AVE REGINA COELORUM

*Es ist ein Land Verloren . . .*

There is a land called Lost
at peace inside our heads.
The moon, full on the frost,
vivifies these stone heads.

Moods of the verb 'to stare',
split selfhoods, conjugate
ice-facets from the air,
the light glazing the light.

Look at us, Queen of Heaven.
Our solitudes drift by
your solitudes, the seven
dead stars in your sky.

## 2 TE LUCIS ANTE TERMINUM

*Wir gehen dir, Heimat, ins Garn . . .*

Centaury with your staunch bloom
you there alder beech you fern,
midsummer closeness my far home,
fresh traces of lost origin.

Silvery the black cherries hang,
the plum-tree oozes through each cleft
and horse-flies siphon the green dung,
glued to the sweetness of their graft:

immortal transience, a 'kind
of otherness', self-understood,
BE FAITHFUL grows upon the mind
as lichen glimmers on the wood.

# A PRE-RAPHAELITE
# NOTEBOOK

Primroses; salutations; the miry skull
of a half-eaten ram; viscous wounds in earth
opening. What seraphs are afoot.

Gold seraph to gold worm in the pierced slime:
greetings. Advent of power-in-grace. The power
of flies distracts the working of our souls.

Earth's abundance. The God-ejected Word
resorts to flesh, procures carrion, satisfies
its white hunger. Salvation's travesty

a deathless metaphor: the stale head
sauced in original blood; the little feast
foaming with cries of rapture and despair.

# TERRIBILIS EST LOCUS ISTE
## Gauguin and the Pont-Aven School

Briefly they are amazed. The marigold-fields
mell and shudder and the travellers,
in sudden exile burdened with remote
hieratic gestures, journey to no end

beyond the vivid severance of each day,
strangeness at doors, a different solitude
between the mirror and the window, marked
visible absences, colours of the mind,

marginal angels lightning-sketched in red
chalk on the month's accounts or marigolds
in paint runnily embossed, or the renounced
self-portrait with a seraph and a storm.

# VENI CORONABERIS

*A Garland for Helen Waddell*


The crocus armies from the dead
rise up; the realm of love renews
the battle it was born to lose,
though for a time the snows have fled

and old stones blossom in the south
with sculpted vine and psaltery
and half-effaced adultery
the bird-dung dribbling from its mouth;

and abstinence crowns all our care
with martyr-laurels for this day.
Towers and steeples rise away
into the towering gulfs of air.

# FLORENTINES

Horses, black-lidded mouths peeled back
to white: well-groomed these warriors ride,
their feuds forgotten, remembered, forgotten . . .
a cavalcade passing, night not far-off;
the stricken faces damnable and serene.

# 'CHRISTMAS TREES'

Bonhoeffer in his skylit cell
bleached by the flares' candescent fall,
pacing out his own citadel,

restores the broken themes of praise,
encourages our borrowed days,
by logic of his sacrifice.

Against wild reasons of the state
his words are quiet but not too quiet.
We hear too late or not too late.

# TENEBRAE

He was so tired that he was scarcely able to
hear a note of the songs: he felt imprisoned
in a cold region where his brain was numb
and his spirit was isolated.


I

Requite this angel whose
flushed and thirsting face
stoops to the sacrifice
out of which it arose.
This is the lord Eros
of grief who pities
no one; it is
Lazarus with his sores.


2

And you, who with your soft but searching voice
drew me out of the sleep where I was lost,
who held me near your heart that I might rest
confiding in the darkness of your choice:
possessed by you I chose to have no choice,
fulfilled in you I sought no further quest.
You keep me, now, in dread that quenches trust,
in desolation where my sins rejoice.
As I am passionate so you with pain
turn my desire; as you seem passionless
so I recoil from all that I would gain,
wounding myself upon forgetfulness,
false ecstasies, which you in truth sustain
as you sustain each item of your cross.

3

Veni Redemptor, but not in our time.
Christus Resurgens, quite out of this world.
'Ave' we cry; the echoes are returned.
Amor Carnalis is our dwelling-place.


4

O light of light, supreme delight;
grace on our lips to our disgrace.
Time roosts on all such golden wrists;
our leanness is our luxury.
Our love is what we love to have;
our faith is in our festivals.


5

Stupefying images of grief-in-dream,
succubae to my natural grief of heart,
cling to me, then; you who will not desert
your love nor lose him in some blank of time.
You come with all the licence of her name
to tell me you are mine. But you are not
and she is not. Can my own breath be hurt
by breathless shadows groaning in their game?
It can. The best societies of hell
acknowledge this, aroused by what they know:
consummate rage recaptured there in full
as faithfulness demands it, blow for blow,
and rectitude that mimics its own fall
reeling with sensual abstinence and woe.

6

This is the ash-pit of the lily-fire,
this is the questioning at the long tables,
this is true marriage of the self-in-self,
this is a raging solitude of desire,
this is the chorus of obscene consent,
this is a single voice of purest praise.


7

He wounds with ecstasy. All
the wounds are his own.
He wears the martyr's crown.
He is the Lord of Misrule.
He is the Master of the Leaping Figures,
the motley factions.
Revelling in auguries
he is the Weeper of the Valedictions.


8

Music survives, composing her own sphere,
Angel of Tones, Medusa, Queen of the Air,
and when we would accost her with real cries
silver on silver thrills itself to ice.

# HYMNS TO OUR LADY OF CHARTRES

I

Eia, with handbells, jews' harps, risible
tuckets of salutation! Otherwise
gnashing and gnawing sound out your praise.
Salve regina! Visible, invisible,

powers, presences, in and beyond the blue
glass, radiantly-occluded Sion, pour
festal light at the feet of the new poor,
scavengers upon grace, and of your true

servant Péguy who cries out from the crowd
where your bienpensants clatter to adore
la Dame du Pilier and her wooden stare.
The priests go nodding by, dainty and shrewd,

and virgins with trim lamps devoutly oiled,
to do the honours of your mysteries.
Through what straits might we come to worship this,
and kneel before you, and be reconciled,

among the flowering lances, the heathen
gold phalanxes of flame; at the high seats
where Mercy is redeemed from its own threats;
with dumb-struck martyrs trumpeted to heaven?

Eia ergo. For this is Sion's twin city
or city-in-law. Across France the great west
windows are full of the sun's holocaust,
the dying blazons of eternity

secured in mazy lead and bevelled stone.
Outside the glass, pigeons rancid as gulls
roost in their stucco-dung on the tiered sills.
The candles blur the air before your throne.

Love is at odds. Your beauty has gone out
so many times; too vividly has flared
through the mild dreams of Herod undeterred.
Your eyes are like the eyes of the devout,

O dulcis Virgo. You are the stained world's
ransom, bear its image, live through your
perpetual exile in its courts of prayer.
'This is the carnal rose that re-enfolds

heaven into earth.' They say you are disposed
to acts of grace: tumblers and holy fools.
Child-saints rejoice you, small immaculate souls,
and mundane sorrows mystically espoused.

3

Redemptrice of all vows and fealties, Dame
de Sous-Terre, pray for us, pitched beneath
your mantle, the limestone and sifted earth
of Beauce. Assoil your lordly vassals; some

mettled by virtue, briskly taking Christ,
and some as captives; those to whom the kiss
of peace was torment in the midst of mass,
those who salute you with a raised fist.

Spes nostra, salve! Your strange countenance
is our remaking. Turn, then, its remote
familial smile upon this Christian rote.
Sly innocence of the blood seized in a trance

by violent knowledge – what it is to know
our strength! Pray for those neophytes who found
in you the source of life, their secret wound.
The seraphim with stark pinions aglow

look blankly at us: we who may be spared,
as well as other ecstasies, the hues
of burning and the damned at their old cries,
your varied mercies, variously adored.

# THE MYSTERY OF THE CHARITY OF
## CHARLES PÉGUY

Crack of a starting-pistol. Jean Jaurès
dies in a wine-puddle. Who or what stares
through the café-window crêped in powder-smoke?
The bill for the new farce reads *Sleepers Awake*.

History commands the stage wielding a toy gun,
rehearsing another scene. It has raged so before,
countless times; and will do, countless times more,
in the guise of supreme clown, dire tragedian.

In Brutus' name martyr and mountebank
ghost Caesar's ghost, his wounds of air and ink
painlessly spouting. Jaurès' blood lies stiff
on menu-card, shirt-front and handkerchief.

Did Péguy kill Jaurès? Did he incite
the assassin? Must men stand by what they write
as by their camp-beds or their weaponry
or shell-shocked comrades while they sag and cry?

Would Péguy answer – stubbornly on guard
among the *Cahiers*, with his army cape
and steely pince-nez and his hermit's beard,
brooding on conscience and embattled hope?

Truth's pedagogue, braving an entrenched class
of fools and scoundrels, children of the world,
his eyes caged and hostile behind glass –
still Péguy said that Hope is a little child.

Violent contrariety of men and days; calm
juddery bombardment of a silent film
showing such things: its canvas slashed with rain
and St Elmo's fire. Victory of the machine!

The brisk celluloid clatters through the gate;
the cortège of the century dances in the street;
and over and over the jolly cartoon
armies of France go reeling towards Verdun.

Rage and regret are tireless to explain
stratagems of the out-manoeuvred man,
the charge and counter-charge. You know the drill,
raw veteran, poet with the head of a bull.

Footslogger of genius, skirmisher with grace
and ill-luck, sentinel of the sacrifice,
without vantage of vanity, though mortal-proud,
defend your first position to the last word.

The sun-tanned earth is your centurion;
you are its tribune. On the hard-won
high places the old soldiers of old France
crowd like good children wrapped in obedience

and sleep, and ready to be taken home.
Whatever that vision, it is not a child's;
it is what a child's vision can become.
Memory, Imagination, harvesters of those fields,

our gifts are spoils, our virtues epitaphs,
our substance is the grass upon the graves.
'Du calme, mon vieux, du calme.' How studiously
one cultivates the sugars of decay,

pâtisserie-tinklings of angels ''sieur-'dame',
the smile of the dead novice in its plush frame,
while greed and disaffection are ingrained
like chalk-dust in the ranklings of the mind.

'Rather the Marne than the *Cahiers*.' True enough,
you took yourself off. Dying, your whole life
fell into place. ''Sieurs-'dames, this is the wall
where he leaned and rested, this is the well

from which he drank.' Péguy, you mock us now.
History takes the measure of your brow
in blank-eyed bronze, brave mediocre work
of *Niclausse, sculpteur*, cornered in the park

among the stout dogs and lame patriots
and all those ghosts, far-gazing in mid-stride,
rising from where they fell, still on parade,
covered in glory and the blood of beetroots.


3

Vistas of richness and reward. The cedar
uprears its lawns of black cirrus. You have found
hundred-fold return though in the land
of exile. You are Joseph the Provider;

and in the fable this is your proper home;
three sides of a courtyard where the bees thrum
in the crimped hedges and the pigeons flirt
and paddle, and sunlight pierces the heart-

shaped shutter-patterns in the afternoon,
shadows of fleurs-de-lys on the stone floors.
Here life is labour and pastime and orison
like something from a simple book of hours;

and immortality, your measured task,
inscribes its antique scars on the new desk
among your relics, bits of ivory quartz
and dented snuffbox won at Austerlitz.

The proofs pile up; the dead are made alive
to their posthumous fame. Here is the archive
of your stewardship; here is your true domaine,
its fields of discourse ripening to the Marne.

Chateau de Trie is yours, Chartres is yours,
and the carved knight of Gisors with the hound;
Colombey-les-deux-Eglises; St Cyr's
cadres and echelons are yours to command.

Yours is their dream of France, militant-pastoral:
musky red gillyvors, the wicker bark
of clematis braided across old brick
and the slow chain that cranks into the well

morning and evening. It is Domrémy
restored; the mystic strategy of Foch
and Bergson with its time-scent, dour panache
deserving of martyrdom. It is an army

of poets, converts, vine-dressers, men skilled
in wood or metal, peasants from the Beauce,
terse teachers of Latin and those unschooled
in all but the hard rudiments of grace.

Such dreams portend, the dreamer prophesies,
is this not true? Truly, if you are wise,
deny such wisdom; bid the grim bonne-femme
defend your door: 'M'sieur is not at home.'


4

This world is different, belongs to them –
the lords of limit and of contumely.
It matters little whether you go tamely
or with rage and defiance to your doom.

This is your enemies' country which they took
in the small hours an age before you woke,
went to the window, saw the mist-hewn
statues of the lean kine emerge at dawn.

Outflanked again, too bad! You still have pride,
haggard obliquities: those that take remorse
and the contempt of others for a muse,
bound to the alexandrine as to the *Code*

*Napoléon*. Thus the bereaved soul returns
upon itself, grows resolute at chess,
in war-games hurling dice of immense loss
into the breach; thus punitively mourns.

This is no old Beauce manoir that you keep
but the rue de la Sorbonne, the cramped shop,
its unsold *Cahiers* built like barricades,
its fierce disciples, disciplines and feuds,

the camelot-cry of 'sticks!' As Tharaud says,
'all through your life the sound of broken glass.'
So much for Jaurès murdered in cold pique
by some vexed shadow of the belle époque,

some guignol strutting at the window-frame.
But what of you, Péguy, who came to 'exult',
to be called 'wolfish' by your friends? The guilt
belongs to time; and you must leave on time.

Jaurès was killed blindly, yet with reason:
'let us have drums to beat down his great voice.'
So you spoke to the blood. So, you have risen
above all that and fallen flat on your face

5

among the beetroots, where we are constrained
to leave you sleeping and to step aside
from the fleshed bayonets, the fusillade
of red-rimmed smoke like stubble being burned;

to turn away and contemplate the working
of the radical soul – instinct, intelligence,
memory, call it what you will – waking
into the foreboding of its inheritance,

its landscape and inner domain; images
of earth and grace. Across Artois the rois-mages
march on Bethlehem; sun-showers fall
slantwise over the kalefield, the canal.

Hedgers and ditchers, quarrymen, thick-shod
curés de campagne, each with his load,
shake off those cares and burdens; they become,
in a bleak visionary instant, seraphim

looking towards Chartres, the spired sheaves,
stone-thronged annunciations, winged ogives
uplifted and uplifting from the winter-gleaned
furrows of that criss-cross-trodden ground.

Or say it is Pentecost: the hawthorn-tree,
set with coagulate magnified flowers of may,
blooms in a haze of light; old chalk-pits brim
with seminal verdure from the roots of time.

Landscape is like revelation; it is both
singular crystal and the remotest things.
Cloud-shadows of seasons revisit the earth,
odourless myrrh borne by the wandering kings.

Happy are they who, under the gaze of God,
die for the 'terre charnelle', marry her blood
to theirs, and, in strange Christian hope, go down
into the darkness of resurrection,

into sap, ragwort, melancholy thistle,
almondy meadowsweet, the freshet-brook
rising and running through small wilds of oak,
past the elder-tump that is the child's castle.

Inevitable high summer, richly scarred
with furze and grief; winds drumming the fame
of the tin legions lost in haystack and stream.
Here the lost are blest, the scarred most sacred:

odd village workshops grimed and peppercorned
in a dust of dead spiders, paper-crowned
sunflowers with the bleached heads of rag dolls,
brushes in aspic, clay pots, twisted nails;

the clinking anvil and clear sheepbell-sound,
at noon and evening, of the angelus;
coifed girls like geese, labourers cap in hand,
and walled gardens espaliered with angels;

solitary bookish ecstasies, proud tears,
proud tears, for the forlorn hope, the guerdon
of Sedan, 'oh les braves gens!', English Gordon
stepping down sedately into the spears.

Patience hardens to a pittance, courage
unflinchingly declines into sour rage,
the cobweb-banners, the shrill bugle-bands
and the bronze warriors resting on their wounds.

These fatal decencies, they make us lords
over ourselves: familial debts and dreads,
keepers of old scores, the kindly ones
telling their beady sous, the child-eyed crones

who guard the votive candles and the faint
invalid's night-light of the sacrament,
a host of lilies and the table laid
for early mass from which you stood aside

to find salvation, your novena cleaving
brusquely against the grain of its own myth,
its truth and justice, to a kind of truth,
a justice hard to justify. 'Having

spoken his mind he'd a mind to be silent.'
But who would credit that, that one talent
dug from the claggy Beauce and returned to it
with love, honour, suchlike bitter fruit?


6


To dispense, with justice; or, to dispense
with justice. Thus the catholic god of France,
with honours all even, honours all, even
the damned in the brazen Invalides of Heaven.

Here there should be a section without words
for military band alone: 'Sambre et Meuse',
the 'Sidi Brahim' or 'Le Roi s'Amuse';
white gloves and monocles and polished swords

and Dreyfus with his buttons off, chalk-faced
but standing to attention, the school prig
caught in some act and properly disgraced.
A puffy satrap prances on one leg

to snap the traitor's sword, his ordered rage
bursting with 'cran et gloire' and gouts of rouge.
The chargers click and shiver. There is no stir
in the drawn ranks, among the hosts of the air,

all draped and gathered by the weird storm-light
cheap wood-engravings cast on those who fought
at Mars-la-Tour, Sedan; or on the men
in the world-famous stories of Jules Verne

or nailed at Golgotha. Drumrap and fife
hit the right note: 'A mort le Juif! Le Juif
à la lanterne!' Serenely the mob howls,
its silent mouthings hammered into scrolls

torn from *Apocalypse*. No wonder why
we fall to violence out of apathy,
redeemed by falling and restored to grace
beyond the dreams of mystic avarice.

But who are 'we', since history is law,
clad in our skins of silver, steel and hide,
or in our rags, with rotten teeth askew,
heroes or knaves as Clio shall decide?

'We' are crucified Pilate, Caiaphas
in his thin soutane and Judas with the face
of a man who has drunk wormwood. We come
back empty-handed from Jerusalem

counting our blessings, honestly admire
the wrath of the peacemakers, for example
Christ driving the money-changers from the temple,
applaud the Roman steadiness under fire.

We are the occasional just men who sit
in gaunt self-judgment on their self-defeat,
the élite hermits, secret orators
of an old faith devoted to new wars.

We are 'embusqués', having no wounds to show
save from the thorns, ecstatic at such pain.
Once more the truth advances; and again
the metaphors of blood begin to flow.


7


Salute us all, Christus with your iron
garlands of poppies and ripe carrion.
No, sleep where you stand; let some boy-officer
take up your vigil with your dungfork spear.

What vigil is this, then, among the polled
willows, cart-shafts uptilted against skies,
translucent rain at jutting calvaries;
on paths that are rutted and broken-walled?

What is this relic fumbled with such care
by mittened fingers in dugout or bomb-
tattered, jangling estaminet's upper room?
The incense from a treasured tabatière,

you watchmen at the Passion. Péguy said
'why do I write of war? Simply because
I have not been there. In time I shall cease
to invoke it.' We still dutifully read

'heureux ceux qui sont morts'. Drawn on the past
these presences endure; they have not ceased
to act, suffer, crouching into the hail
like labourers of their own memorial

or those who worship at its marble rote,
their many names one name, the common 'dur'
built into duration, the endurance of war;
blind Vigil herself, helpless and obdurate.

And yet what sights: Saul groping in the dust
for his broken glasses, or the men far-gone
on the road to Emmaus who saw the ghost.
Commit all this to memory. The line

falters, reforms, vanishes into the smoke
of its own unknowing; mother, dad,
gone in that shell-burst, with the other dead,
'pour la patrie', according to the book.

## 8

Dear lords of life, stump-toothed, with ragged breath,
throng after throng cast out upon the earth,
flesh into dust, who slowly come to use
dreams of oblivion in lieu of paradise,

push on, push on! – through struggle, exhaustion,
indignities of all kinds, the impious Christian
oratory, 'vos morituri', through berserk fear,
laughing, howling, 'servitude et grandeur'

in other words, in nameless gobbets thrown
up by the blast, names issuing from mouths
of the dying, with their dying breaths.
But rest assured, bristly-brave gentlemen

of Normandie and Loire. Death does you proud,
every heroic commonplace, 'Amor',
'Fidelitas', polished like old armour,
stamped forever into the featureless mud.

Poilus and sous-officiers who plod
to your lives' end, name your own recompense,
expecting nothing but the grace of France,
drawn to her arms, her august plenitude.

The blaze of death goes out, the mind leaps
for its salvation, is at once extinct;
its last thoughts tetter the furrows, distinct
in dawn twilight, caught on the barbed loops.

Whatever strikes and maims us it is not
fate, to our knowledge. En avant, Péguy!
The irony of advancement. Say 'we
possess nothing; try to hold on to that.'

## 9

There is an ancient landscape of green branches –
true tempérament de droite, you have your wish –
crosshatching twigs and light, goldfinches
among the peppery lilac, the small fish

pencilled into the stream. Ah, such a land
the Ile de France once was. Virelai and horn
wind through the meadows, the dawn-masses sound
fresh triumphs for our Saviour crowned with scorn.

Good governors and captains, by your leave,
you also were sore-wounded but those wars
are ended. Iron men who bell the hours,
marshals of porte-cochère and carriage-drive,

this is indeed perfection, this is the heart
of the mystère. Yet one would not suppose
Péguy's 'defeat', 'affliction', your lost cause.
Old Bourbons view-hallooing for regret

among the cobwebs and the ghostly wine,
you dream of warrior-poets and the Meuse
flowing so sweetly; the androgynous Muse
your priest-confessor, sister-châtelaine.

How the mood swells to greet the gathering storm!
The chestnut trees begin to thresh and cast
huge canisters of blossom at each gust.
Coup de tonnerre! Bismarck is in the room!

Bad memories, seigneurs? Such wraiths appear
on summer evenings when the gnat-swarm spins
a dying moment on the tremulous air.
The curtains billow and the rain begins

its night-long vigil. Sombre heartwoods gleam,
the clocks replenish the small hours' advance
and not a soul has faltered from its trance.
'Je est un autre', that fatal telegram,

floats past you in the darkness, unreceived.
Connoisseurs of obligation, history
stands, a blank instant, awaiting your reply:
'If we but move a finger France is saved!'


10

Down in the river-garden a grey-gold
dawnlight begins to silhouette the ash.
A rooster wails remotely over the marsh
like Mr Punch mimicking a lost child.

At Villeroy the copybook lines of men
rise up and are erased. Péguy's cropped skull
dribbles its ichor, its poor thimbleful,
a simple lesion of the complex brain.

Woefully battered but not too bloody,
smeared by fraternal root-crops and at one
with the fritillary and the veined stone,
having composed his great work, his small body,

for the last rites of truth, whatever they are,
or the Last Judgment which is much the same,
or Mercy, even, with her tears and fire,
he commends us to nothing, leaves a name

for the burial-detail to gather up
with rank and number, personal effects,
the next-of-kin and a few other facts;
his arm over his face as though in sleep

or to ward off the sun: the body's prayer,
the tribute of his true passion, for Chartres
steadfastly cleaving to the Beauce, for her,
the Virgin of innumerable charities.

'Encore plus douloureux et doux.' Note how
sweetness devours sorrow, renders it again,
turns to affliction each more carnal pain.
Whatever is fulfilled is now the law

where law is grace, that grace won by inches,
inched years. The men of sorrows do their stint,
whose golgothas are the moon's trenches,
the sun's blear flare over the salient.

J'accuse! j'accuse! – making the silver prance
and curvet, and the dust-motes jig to war
across the shaky vistas of old France,
the gilt-edged maps of Strasbourg and the Saar.

Low tragedy, high farce, fight for command,
march, counter-march, and come to the salute
at every hole-and-corner burial-rite
bellowed with hoarse dignity into the wind.

Take that for your example! But still mourn,
being so moved: éloge and elegy
so moving on the scene as if to cry
'in memory of those things these words were born.'

# NOTES AND ACKNOWLEDGEMENTS

The present volume reprints all the poems from my five individual books of verse, together with the three 'Hymns to Our Lady of Chartres' which are here appearing in print for the first time. The earliest of the poems, 'Genesis', dates from 1952. The 'Hymns . . .' were composed in 1983–4 shortly after the completion of *The Mystery of the Charity of Charles Péguy*. They are placed out of chronological sequence because I wish the book to conclude with that poem: 'in memory of those things these words were born'.

I have felt impelled to alter words and phrases here and there. I have changed only those details which have become a burden over the years.

The second epigraph is from *Situations*, reprinted by permission of Editions Gallimard, Paris.
The third epigraph is a line from 'Canto 11', reprinted from *The Cantos of Ezra Pound* by permission of Faber & Faber Ltd.

# FOR THE UNFALLEN (1959)

The six lines from 'More Sonnets at Christmas, 1942' are quoted from *Poems 1920–1945: A Selection* (1947) by Allen Tate, by kind permission of Eyre & Spottiswoode (Publishers) Ltd and Charles Scribners' Sons.

# KING LOG (1968)

## FUNERAL MUSIC: AN ESSAY

In this sequence I was attempting a florid grim music broken by grunts and shrieks. Ian Nairn's description of Eltham Palace as 'a perfect example of the ornate heartlessness of much mid-fifteenth-century architecture, especially court architecture'[1] is pertinent, though I did not read Nairn until after the sequence had been completed. The Great Hall was made for Edward IV. *Funeral Music* could be called a commination and an alleluia for the period popularly but inexactly known as the Wars of the Roses. It bears an oblique dedication. In the case of Suffolk the word 'beheaded' is a retrospective aggrandisement; he was in fact butchered across the gunwale of a skiff. Tiptoft enjoyed a degree of ritual, commanding that he should be decapitated in three strokes 'in honour of the Trinity'. This was a nice compounding of orthodox humility and unorthodox arrogance. Did Tiptoft see himself as Everyman's emblem or as the unique figure preserved in the tableau of his own death? As historic characters Suffolk, Worcester and Rivers haunt the mind vulnerable alike to admiration and scepticism. Was Suffolk – the friend of the captive poet Charles d'Orleans and an advocate of peace with France – a visionary or a racketeer? The Woodville clan invites irritated dismissal: pushful, time-serving, it was really not its business to produce a man like Earl Rivers, who was something of a religious mystic and whose translation, *The Dictes and Sayings of the Philosophers*, was the first book printed in England by Caxton. Suffolk and Rivers were poets, though quite tame. Tiptoft, patron of humanist scholars, was known as the Butcher of England because of his pleasure in varying the accepted postures of judicial death.

Admittedly, the sequence avoids shaping these characters and events into any overt narrative or dramatic structure. The whole inference, though, has value if it gives a key to the ornate and heartless music punctuated by mutterings, blasphemies and cries for help.

There is a distant fury of battle. Without attempting factual detail, I had in mind the Battle of Towton, fought on Palm Sunday, 1461. It is now customary to play down the violence of the Wars of the Roses and to present them as dynastic skirmishes fatal, perhaps, to the old aristocracy but generally of small concern to the common people and without much effect on the economic routines of the kingdom. Statistically, this may be arguable; imaginatively, the Battle of Towton itself commands one's belated witness. In the accounts of the contemporary chroniclers it was a holocaust. Some scholars have suggested that the claims were exagger-

[1] Ian Nairn, *Nairn's London* (1966), p. 208

ated, although the military historian, Colonel A. H. Burne, argues convincingly for the reasonableness of the early estimates. He reckons that over twenty-six thousand men died at Towton and remarks that 'the scene must have beggared description and its very horror probably deterred the survivors from passing on stories of the fight'.[2] Even so, one finds the chronicler of Croyland Abbey writing that the blood of the slain lay caked with the snow which covered the ground and that, when the snow melted, the blood flowed along the furrows and ditches for a distance of two or three miles.[3]


# MERCIAN HYMNS (1971)

The historical King Offa reigned over Mercia (and the greater part of England south of the Humber) in the years AD 757–96. During early medieval times he was already becoming a creature of legend. The Offa who figures in this sequence might perhaps most usefully be regarded as the presiding genius of the West Midlands, his dominion enduring from the middle of the eighth century until the middle of the twentieth (and possibly beyond). The indication of such a timespan will, I trust, explain and to some extent justify a number of anachronisms.

I have a duty to acknowledge that the authorities cited in these notes might properly object to their names being used in so unscholarly and fantastic a context. I have no wish to compromise the accurate scholarship of others. Having taken over certain statements and references from my reading and having made them a part of the idiom of this sequence, I believe that I should acknowledge the sources. I have specified those debts of which I am aware. Possibly there are others of which I am unaware. If that is so I regret the oversight.

The title of the sequence is a suggestion taken from *Sweet's Anglo-Saxon Reader* (1950 edn), pp. 170–80. A less-immediate precedent is provided by the Latin prose-hymns or canticles of the early Christian

---

[2] A. H. Burne, *The Battlefields of England* (1950), p. 100
[3] Cited by C. R. Markham, *The Yorkshire Archaeological and Topographical Journal*, Vol. 10 (1889), p. 13

Church. See Frederick Brittain, ed., *The Penguin Book of Latin Verse* (1962), pp. xvii, lv.

II: 'a common name' cf. W. F. Bolton, *A History of Anglo-Latin Literature 597–1066* (1967), Vol. I, p. 191: 'But Offa is a common name'.

IV: 'I was invested in mother-earth'. To the best of my recollection, the expression 'to invest in mother-earth' was the felicitous (and correct) definition of 'yird' given by Mr (now Sir) Michael Hordern in the programme *Call My Bluff* televised on BBC 2 on Thursday 29 January 1970.

V: 'wergild': 'the price set upon a man according to his rank' (OED) cf. D. Whitelock, *The Beginnings of English Society* (1965 edn), ch. 5.

XI: *'Offa Rex'*: an inscription on his coins. See J. J. North, *English Hammered Coinage* (1963), Vol. I, pp. 52–60 and Plate III.

XIII: *'Rex Totius Anglorum Patriae'*: 'King of the Whole Country of the English'. See Christopher Brooke, *The Saxon and Norman Kings* (1967 edn), p. 200.

XV: 'Cernunnos': cf. *Larousse Encyclopedia of Mythology* (1960 edn), pp. 235, 244, 246–8.

XVII: *'haleine'*: cf. *La Chanson de Roland*, ed. F. Whitehead (1942), 1789, 'Ço dist li reis: "Cel corn ad lunge aleine."'

XVIII: 'for consolation and philosophy': the allusion is to the title of Boethius' great meditation, though it is doubtless an excess of scruple to point this out.

'To watch the Tiber foaming out much blood': adapted from Virgil, *Aeneid*, VI, 87, 'et Thybrim multo spumantem sanguine cerno'.

XX: 'Ethandune', 'Catraeth', 'Maldon', 'Pengwern': in this context supposedly the names of English suburban dwellings. Ethandune = the Battle of Edington (Wilts), AD 878; Catraeth = the Battle of Catterick, late sixth century; Maldon = the Battle of Maldon, AD 991; Pengwern (Shrewsbury), capital of the Princes of Powys, taken by Offa, AD 779. See Anthony Conran, ed., *The Penguin Book of Welsh Verse* (1967), pp. 24–30, 75–78, 90–93; Richard Hamer, ed., *A Choice of Anglo-Saxon*

*Verse* (1970), pp. 48–69; A. H. Smith, ed., *The Parker Chronicle* (1951 edn), pp. 31–2.

XXIII: *'Opus Anglicanum'*: the term is properly applicable to English embroidery of the period AD 1250–1350, though the craft was already famous some centuries earlier. See A. G. I. Christie, *English Medieval Embroidery* (1938), pp. 1–2. In XXIV and XXV I have, with considerable impropriety, extended the term to apply to English Romanesque sculpture and to utilitarian metal-work of the nineteenth century.

XXIV: for the association of Compostela with West Midlands sculpture of the twelfth century I am indebted to G. Zarnecki, *Later English Romanesque Sculpture* (1953), esp. pp. 9–15, 'The Herefordshire School'.

'Et exspecto resurrectionem mortuorum': a debt to Olivier Messiaen, his music 'for orchestra of woodwind, brass and metallic percussion'.

XXV: 'the eightieth letter of *Fors Clavigera*'. See *The Works of John Ruskin* (1903–1912), Vol. XXIX, pp. 170–80.

'darg': 'a day's work, the task of a day . . .' (OED). Ruskin employs the word, here and elsewhere.

'quick forge': see W. Shakespeare, *Henry V*, v, Chorus, 23. The phrase requires acknowledgement but the source has no bearing on the poem.

'wire': I seem not to have been strictly accurate. Hand-made nails were forged from rods. Wire was used for the 'French nails' made by machine. But: 'wire' = 'metal wrought into the form of a slender rod or thread' (OED).

XXVII: 'Now when King Offa was alive and dead' is based on a ritual phrase used of various kings though not, as far as I am aware, of Offa himself. See Christopher Brooke, *op. cit.*, p. 39; R. H. M. Dolley, ed., *Anglo-Saxon Coins: Studies Presented to F. M. Stenton* (1961), p. 220.

# TENEBRAE (1978)

Spanish and German poems have provided points of departure for several poems in this book. 'The Pentecost Castle' is particularly indebted to J. M. Cohen's *The Penguin Book of Spanish Verse*. The final sonnet of 'Lachrimae' is a free translation of a sonnet by Lope de Vega (Cohen, p. 247) and the second sonnet of 'An Apology . . .' is an imitation of a sonnet by L. L. de Argensola (Cohen, p. 202). The poems by Paul Celan on which I have based my 'Two Chorale-Preludes' are from *Die Niemandsrose* (1963): 'Eis, Eden' and 'Kermorvan'. I have combined a few phrases of free translation with phrases of my own invention.

'A Pre-Raphaelite Notebook' adapts a sentence from Pascal's *Pensées*. The last line of 'Quaint Mazes' is indebted to Ronald Blythe, 'Satan without Seraphs' in the *Listener*, 4 February 1971. 'Te Lucis Ante Terminum' quotes a phrase from Walter J. Ong S.J., 'Voice as Summons for Belief' (*Literature and Belief: English Institute Essays* (1957) 1958, p. 84). 'A Short History of British India (I)': see S. P. Carey, *William Carey* (1934 edn), p. 101.

I gratefully acknowledge the permission of Oxford University Press for the quotations from Imogen Holst, *The Music of Gustav Holst* (2nd edn, 1968), and Simone Weil, *First and Last Notebooks* translated by Richard Rees, 1970; and of A. P. Watt Ltd for the quotation from *The Letters of W. B. Yeats*, ed. Allan Wade (1954).

# THE MYSTERY OF THE CHARITY OF CHARLES PÉGUY (1983)

2.1: 'poet with the head of a bull': *Poetry*, a tapestry by Jean Lurçat, depicts the twelve signs of the zodiac and a poet with the head of a bull.

2.7: '"Rather the Marne than the *Cahiers*"': adapts a phrase from a review-article by P. McCarthy, TLS, 16 June, 1978, p. 675.

4.1: 'the lords of limit': The phrase is Auden's, from an early poem 'Now from my window-sill I watch the night'. See Edward Mendelson, ed., *The English Auden* (1977), pp. 115–16.

4.6: 'the camelot-cry of "sticks!"': *Les camelots du roi* was a right-wing, anti-Dreyfusard organization, prominent in the street-battles of the period.

4.6: 'As Tharaud says': Daniel Halévy, *Péguy and 'Les Cahiers de la Quinzaine'*, translated from the French by Ruth Bethell (1946), p. 171: 'Always, all through his life, this sound of broken glass, to use Tharaud's expression'.

5.8: 'die for the "terre charnelle"'; Charles Péguy, *Ève* (1913): '– Heureux ceux qui sont morts pour la terre charnelle, / Mais pourvu que se fût dans une juste guerre.'

9.1: 'true tempérament de droite, you have your wish': See Robert Speaight, *Georges Bernanos* (1973), p. 36, for 'what Jacques Maritain has called a *tempérament de droite*'. See also pp. 17–18 for Speaight's view of the great similarities, as well as the great differences, between Bernanos and Péguy.

9.8: '"Je est un autre", that fatal telegram': Arthur Rimbaud, *Lettre à Georges Izambard*, May 1871: 'vous ne comprendrez pas du tout, et je ne saurais presque vous expliquer . . . *Je* est un autre . . .'

10.7: 'Encore plus douloureux et doux': from a quatrain by Charles Péguy.

10.11: 'in memory of those things these words were born': adapts a sentence from Marcel Raymond, *From Baudelaire to Surrealism* (1961), p. 190: referring to Péguy's 'Présentation de la Beauce à Notre-Dame de Chartres'.


CHARLES PÉGUY

Charles Péguy was born in 1873 into a family of barely-literate peasants, to whom he subsequently devoted much eloquent homage, and died, an ageing infantry lieutenant of the Reserve, on the first day of the first Battle of the Marne in September 1914. He was a son of the people, of 'l'ancienne France', one of the last of that race as he conceived of it. His reputation, such as it was during his lifetime, was confined to a small intellectual élite: the few hundred readers of *Les Cahiers de la Quinzaine*, which he founded in 1900, and the dozen or so who attended the

Thursday meetings in his little bookshop, the 'Boutique des Cahiers', in the shadow of the Sorbonne. A man of the most exact and exacting probity, accurate practicality, in personal and business relations, a meticulous reader of proof, he was at the same time moved by violent emotions and violently afflicted by mischance. Like others similarly wounded, he was perhaps smitten by the desirability of suffering. 'Fils de vaincu, il est attiré par les défaites': such is the suggestion of Simone Fraisse; and a further remark, quoted by Halévy, 'Always, all through his life, this sound of broken glass', felicitously evokes a variety of painful scenes: from the street-battles, the riotous fringe of 'L'Affaire Dreyfus' (that extraordinary collision of two kinds of patriotism, the one cynical, reactionary, the other regenerative and sacrificial) to the harsh severing of old alliances and friendships in the years that followed. A staunchly-committed Dreyfusard, Péguy was an admirer of the great socialist deputy Jean Jaurès throughout the period of the 'Affair'. By 1914 he was calling for his blood: figuratively, it must be said; though a young madman, who may or may not have been over-susceptible to metaphor, almost immediately shot Jaurès through the head.

Péguy had become a socialist during his college days and remained one, though of an increasingly eccentric cast of thought and speech. T. Stearns Eliot, MA (Harvard), who made reference to Péguy's life and work in a series of university extension lectures in 1916, noted that he 'illustrates nationalism and neo-Catholicism as well as socialism', and treated his ideas in close association with those of Georges Sorel. It has been said that 'Péguy's socialism re-emerged as the national-socialism of Barrès and Sorel'; but fascism, in whatever form, is a travesty of Péguy's true faith and position. He did not, in the end, have a great deal in common with Sorel; quarrelled with him; was certainly not anti-semitic.

His brave and timely death in a beetroot field by the Marne transformed this much-snubbed irascible man into the kind of figure-in-profile for whom church and civic dignitaries turn out in force, whose 'essential idea' even Ministers of Education may safely extol.

No one knows for certain whether he did, or did not, receive the sacrament on the Feast of the Assumption, shortly before he was killed. Estranged from the Church for a number of years, first by his militant socialist principles, then by the consequences of a civil marriage, he had, in 1908, rediscovered the solitary ardours of faith but not the consolations of religious practice. He remained self-excommunicate but adoring; his devotion most doggedly expressed in those two pilgrimages undertaken on foot, in June 1912 and July 1913, from Paris to the Cathedral of Notre Dame de Chartres. The purpose of his first journey, as a tablet in the Cathedral duly records, was to entrust his children to Our Lady's care.

There is still a 'Boutique des Cahiers', a handy stone's-throw from the Sorbonne. Its appearance, at least on the outside, seems remarkably unchanged from that preserved by photographs taken in 1902 and 1913 except, of course, that there is now a plaque on the wall. John Middleton Murry, in his autobiography, affords 'a glimpse . . . through the windows of his little shop . . . of a man with a pince-nez set awry on his nose, tying up a parcel: that was Charles Péguy. I admired him, and admire him still.' In this vignette we too glimpse something of the tragi-comic battered élan of Péguy's life. Murry's final cadence is without reservation, and I like him for such an expression of outright admiration. Péguy, stubborn rancours and mishaps and all, is one of the great souls, one of the great prophetic intelligences, of our century. I offer *The Mystery of the Charity of Charles Péguy* as my homage to the triumph of his 'defeat'.